CREATIVITY UNLEASHED

5 HABITS OF WORLD-CLASS INNOVATORS

JONATHAN FANNING

WWW.JONATHANFANNING.COM

Jonathan Fanning

CREATIVITY UNLEASHED

ISBN

Cover Design: Ella Fanning

For more information on this title and other books, videos, coaching programs, and speaking engagements, please visit:

www.JonathanFanning.com

Printed in the United States of America.

Contents

Jonathan Fanning

Creativity Unleashed Blueprint

Do you want more creativity in your life?

Are you sure?

We love creativity. We love innovators… in the rearview mirror. After it's worked – whatever the it happens to be. A few days ago, I walked through a museum dedicated to an artist who created over 2,000 works in his lifetime. He created a new painting or sketch ever day or two. During his lifetime he sold only one. ONE! On the 100th anniversary of his death, Vincent van Gogh's painting, "Portrait of Dr. Gachet", sold for a then world record $82.5 million. Was Van Gogh creative? Was he successful?

Nikola Tesla died broke. He was living on a diet of crackers and milk. In the late 1890s and early 1900s, he had this idea that we could transmit electricity through the airwaves. He tested that idea and it worked. Tesla wanted to deliver electricity wirelessly via satellites in earth's orbit – 7 decades before the lunar landing. Today, you put your phone on a pad and it charges, wirelessly, using Tesla's ideas from 120 years ago. Tesla thought we would be able to communicate via the airwaves with people anywhere in the world, on a device the size of a wristwatch. He died broke. Was Tesla creative? Was he successful?

We love creativity after it's worked! We put innovators on a pedestal, but not always during their lifetimes or in the middle of the creative process.

I ask again, do you really want more creativity in your life?

Why?

Why would you want to be more creative? Seriously. If you had a simple and practical blueprint for unleashing creativity in your life, would you use it? Where would you use it? Career? Starting or growing a business? Relationships? Parenting? Impacting the world around you? How you spend your free time? Finances? Travel?

Vacation? Connection? Learning? Fitness? What if you could share that blueprint with others? Have you ever wished you could help your team, peers, friends and family members to be a little more creative?

Over almost two decades, we studied world-class innovators, looking for practical strategies and habits.

Before we dive in, are you sure that you actually do want more creativity?

In your work… in your relationships… in the way you impact the community… in your finances… in your communication…

With more creativity in your life, what changes?

I've had so many moments when I thought: *I need more creativity!*

In my first job after college, I was in an amazing leadership development program. Each Thursday, we participated in a half day of incredible leadership training sessions. Afterwards, we'd have lunch with a high level leader and get to ask questions. I sat there, Thursday after Thursday thinking several things: 1) I want to get "there" faster 2) What each "successful" leader described didn't sound like success to me. I want something more, better, different. 3) I was convinced that I was supposed to have a positive impact on the world around me – supposed to do more than just have a career or make a living. I had this deep down thought that I was supposed to create a ripple effect. How do you do that?

I was convinced with each passing Thursday that I wanted something different from what most people had. I wanted a greater impact, more time, more purpose, better relationships…I wanted to make a difference AND have time for a great family life. I was also convinced that if you want different results, it would require another level of creativity. I thought I was fairly creative, but I didn't yet see the answers to some of these riddles.

Perhaps you can relate?

How close are you to your creative potential? Are you becoming more creative... or not? It is that simple. What's your answer? Are you more creative today than you were a year ago? Do you have a process for unleashing creativity?

I started looking for answers. What do world-class innovators do differently? What practical strategies can we borrow to raise the lid on our own creativity? When you mention the word creativity or innovation, most of us seem to think of artists, writers, musicians, designers, fashion or trend-setters, marketers, software designers, scientists, chemists, medical researchers, or technology gurus. But creativity applies to so much more. How do you communicate? What happens at your dinner table? What fills your weekend calendar? How do you spend your vacations? How do you learn new concepts? How do you teach or mentor? How do you interact with your friends, family, co-workers? What happens at all those meetings that you get to attend? How do you create financial opportunities for today and tomorrow? In what ways do you give back to the world? How do your charity efforts create a ripple effect that will continue for years? How do you read books? (By the way, please feel free to skip around in this book. This first chapter is a framework for creativity. Each subsequent chapter is self-sufficient, so you can read whatever catches your attention.)

Over the course of two decades, I studied some of the most creative people, leaders, and organizations in the world. Some are world-famous. Most are not. Do world-class innovators have secrets? Can they be discovered? Can they be intentionally implemented, practiced, coached, developed, taught? I discovered a blueprint and started using it and teaching it. I've had the chance now to share the blueprint with audiences around the world, from Australia to the US to Europe.

It works and you can work it. The real question is, What will you do with this blueprint?

Join me as we meet world-class innovators from all walks of life and explore hundreds of very practical application suggestions. We will unpack five simple ways to increase creativity, individually and in the many organizations to which we all belong.

As we uncover powerful strategies for increasing creativity, we come face to face with a deeper question: Do you truly want to become more creative? Are you sure? If you pause for a moment, you may realize what so many of us try not to admit aloud: you're not sure that you want to be more creative. Or, you want to be just a little more creative, once in a while.

Does our culture encourage and reward creativity? Sure! Once the result of that creativity has worked out, we usually do, but not so much before positive results are achieved. The earliest Beatles songs were not recorded! Tesla's early experiments with transmitting electricity through the air waves over a century ago were not embraced. Walt Disney's two follies (before they were successful): Snow White and Disneyland. Mark Twain wisely said, "A person with a new idea is a crank until the idea succeeds." We love creativity, we reward creativity… *once it works!*

What stops us?

In the 1960s, NASA hired George Land to help them assess creativity. NASA wanted a filter to facilitate the selection of the most creative people, so Land built a creativity test. The test was so effective that a modified version was used to test creativity in children. 1,600 children took the test three times over the course of ten years, when they were five-, ten-, and fifteen-years-old. Land also tested hundreds of thousands of adults. The results are a wake-up call. The percentage who scored in the "highly creative" range dropped from 98% at age 5 to 30% at age 10, 12% at age 15, and 2% for adults. What? When I first read these results, I practically screamed, "What did they do to us?" My next response carried similar emotion: "What are you and I doing to young people?" I think Land summarized the assessment best: "What we have concluded is that non-creative behavior is learned." Thank you, NASA and George Land! The vast implications of this non-creative *"training"* may bother you, but the comfort I find is this: if non-creative behavior can be learned, so can creative behavior. We can reverse the process. We can unlearn what we learned or relearn what we unlearned! That's encouraging, albeit not a very fluid sentence. Can I get a few points for creativity here?

Before the un-learning took its toll, when you were five years old, you and I likely shared these significant perspectives:

1. *Question Everything.*
2. *It (anything...) is possible!*
3. *Borrowing is allowed.*
4. *There's not just 1 right answer.*
5. *It's okay to be wrong.*

Before a recent keynote speech in the Midwest, I was in a public restroom washing my hands – or trying to. The water wouldn't turn on. I motioned under the faucet repeatedly and from various angles, but that sensor just wouldn't register to turn the water on. After several tries, a young boy, likely about four, was about to walk past me. He stopped in his tracks, his face took on a highly animated excitement, and he practically shouted, "You just have to wave at it! Like this!" He then proceeded to demonstrate, waving his hands wildly. This small boy didn't worry at all about what I might think of his suggestion. Being "wrong", questioned, or looked at with one of those "of course I've already tried that" expressions didn't even cross his mind. If I ask my youngest daughter, eight-year-old Maya, what she'd like to do on the weekend, she might suggest going to Poland, Pennsylvania, Walt Disney World, Sea World, Germany, and the Washington D.C. Zoo all in the same 48 hours. Borrowing ideas or answers from others is also not a problem for children. I just spoke in Orlando for a national conference and asked the audience to think of a current leadership challenge that requires creativity. I then asked, "How many people have solved a similar problem. Is it hundreds of people? Thousands? Millions?" One executive near the stage had an expression of exasperation. I looked at him, held out my hand, and said, "I bet that at least a million people have solved a version of your current biggest leadership challenge." His facial expression was clear. He did not agree. After my keynote, we had a great conversation. He didn't think that thousands or millions of people had solved his current biggest leadership challenge. I asked what the challenge was. His reply: "Getting my team to work together." I didn't reply right away. When I did, I slowly asked, "Getting a team of people to work together... how many people throughout history have successfully dealt with this challenge?" This very successful executive then looked down for several seconds before a slight smile formed on his face. "We're talking about borrowing ideas here. The answer is probably in the hundreds of millions, perhaps in the billions." By this point, he was laughing and continued, "I have family members who are great at this. Some of the members of my team are much better at getting their teams to work together than I am. I bet every good sports coach in history has a few lessons that I could borrow. Most parents would have a few tips for getting a group of people to work together. The best kindergarten teachers would, as well." How often do we try to solve a problem all alone, without tapping the ideas of the millions who have solved similar problems!

Five Pillars – The Blueprint

There are five distinct things that you and I can focus on during our journey to becoming more creative. The five may sound simple, but the world-class innovators, the masters, the legends, the cultures that live creatively, they do some – or all – of the five a little better and a little more consistently than most of us.

1. Ask: Pursue great questions

2. Expect: Expect to find answers
3. Collect: Collect ideas, perspectives, experiences, options
4. Iterate: "5% Rule" - Model, Modify, Merge, Mash ideas
5. Fail: "F4(OB)" - Fail Forward Fast Frequently (Off Broadway)

Ask: Einstein's Hour

Ask. The greatest innovators ask – more than ask – they *pursue* great questions. The quality of our lives hinges on the quality of the questions we pursue. I'm convinced of this. I see evidence of it everywhere. We all ask good questions now and then, but it's not about the questions we ask now and then. What questions do you pursue? For well over a decade now, I've been pursuing these two questions: Who are you becoming? Who are you helping those around you to become? I started asking the first shortly after a life-altering car accident, which I wrote about in another book, but it wasn't until I started pursuing the question with a tenacity that it would begin to have an impact on my life. Ask great questions. Pursue great questions. Everyone asks great questions occasionally. If you want to radically alter your life, *pursue* some great questions, don't simply ask them.

Practice "Einstein's Hour"! The brilliant Albert Einstein was once asked how he would solve a complicated problem if given just 60 minutes. Einstein's answer: "If I had an hour to solve a problem and my life depended on the solution, I would spend the first 55 minutes determining the proper question to ask, for once I know the proper question, I could solve the problem in less than five minutes." Most of us follow the exact opposite ratio. What's the problem: 5 minutes or LESS... Let's solve it: 55 minutes or more!

Before we get to great questions, let's just start with questioning. Question things around you. In the world of education, Sal Khan, the founder of the Khan Academy, is one of many to question a whole series of assumptions:

- Is a teacher's job to teach or to facilitate learning?
- Is 12 years the ideal length of time for primary school?
- Is 5 the ideal # of learning days per week for all ages?
- How does summer vacation impact learning?
- Does homework have a positive or negative impact on learning? What would amplify its impact?
- Does student-teacher ratio matter or is student to teacher effective interaction ratio more important?
- Since many experts say 70% of kindergartners will start their career in a job that currently does not exist, what preparation matters most?
- Are we holding teachers and schools accountable for what matters most?
- What does matter most in education?

My uncle Bill invested his whole career in public education. He would often say that if kids graduate high school and don't love learning, we have not done our job. That begs the question: Have we done our job?

When my youngest daughter, Maya, was in first grade, I had the opportunity to observe her classroom. After watching an extremely gifted teacher demonstrate a myriad of tools to engage the students, I asked the teacher what questions she pursues. Here are a few of her questions:

- How can I re-energize myself?
- What does Maya (or another of the students) need from me to make this lesson fun, relevant, and memorable?

We'll learn more about Maya's Kindergarten Super-Teacher later in the book.

Can you question a tradition as long-held as America's Past-Time, baseball? Brad Pitt played the role of Billy Beane in the 2011 movie, Moneyball. Pitt's character was based on the general manager for the Oakland A's and he had the audacity to question one of the pillars of professional baseball. In a famous scene, the team has just lost several key players to higher paying teams, including the NY Yankees. A young mathematician, Peter Brand, confronts Billy Beane in the parking garage.

Peter Brand: *There is an epidemic failure within the game to understand what is really happening. And this leads people who run Major League Baseball teams to misjudge their players and mismanage their teams. I apologize.*

Billy Beane: *Go on.*

Peter Brand: *Okay. People who run ball clubs, they think in terms of buying players. Your goal shouldn't be to buy players, your goal should be to buy wins. And in order to buy wins, you need to buy runs. You're trying to replace Johnny Damon. The Boston Red Sox see Johnny Damon and they see a star who's worth seven and half million dollars a year. When I see Johnny Damon, what I see is... is... an imperfect understanding of where runs come from. The guy's got a great glove. He's a decent leadoff hitter. He can steal bases. But is he worth the seven and half million dollars a year that the Boston Red Sox are paying him? No. No. Baseball thinking is medieval. They are asking all the wrong questions. And if I say it to anybody, I'm-I'm ostracized. I'm-I'm-I'm a leper. So that's why I'm-I'm cagey about this with you. That's why I... I respect you, Mr. Beane, and if you want full disclosure, I think it's a good thing that you got Damon off your payroll. I think it opens up all kinds of interesting possibilities.*

Shortly thereafter, Beane has this interaction with his management team:

Management Team: *We're trying to solve the problem here, Billy.*

Billy: *Not like this you're not. You're not even looking at the problem.*

Team: *We're very aware of the problem. I mean...*

Billy: *Okay, good. What's the problem?*

Team: *Look, Billy, we all understand what the problem is. We have to...*

Billy: *Okay, good. What's the problem?*

Team: *The problem is we have to replace three key players in our lineup.*

Billy: *Nope. What's the problem?*

Team: *Same as it's ever been. We've gotta replace these guys with what we have existing.*

Billy: *Nope. What's the problem, Barry?*

Team: *We need 38 home runs, 120 RBIs and 47 doubles to replace.*

Billy: *Ehh!* [imitates buzzer] *The problem we're trying to solve is that there are rich teams and there are poor teams. Then there's fifty feet of crap, and then there's us. It's an unfair game. And now we've been gutted. We're like organ donors for the rich. Boston's taken our kidneys, Yankees have taken our heart. And you guys just sit around talking the same old "good body" nonsense like we're selling jeans. Like we're looking for Fabio. We've got to think differently. We are the last dog at the bowl. You see what happens to the runt of the litter? He dies.*

They're asking all the wrong questions! Billy Beane and Peter Brand go on to significantly change the metrics of professional baseball. Using their approach, Oakland wins 103 games the following season, the same number of games as the NY Yankees, but the price difference is astounding. The Yankees spent $1.4

million *per win*, while Oakland spent $260 thousand *per win*. That equates to almost 5½ times the spending for each win. In many fields, the belief that money turns into results is a self-limiting assumption. Peter Brand might call it medieval. He might say that if you question the "it takes money to make money" or "what can we really do with such a limited budget?" assumptions, you might be ostracized. Would he be right? More to the core, would you and I participate in the ostracizing?

Silicon Valley venture capitalist, Mike Maples, says "Too much money in a startup is not only unnecessary, it's actually toxic." I regularly meet people who are starting a new business or growing a new branch of an existing organization who tell me they wish the budget was bigger. My response is almost always the same. ***Don't wish you had more resources. Wish you were more resourceful. Better yet... Become more resourceful.*** Founder of Honda Motor Corporation, Soichiro Honda, learned early on that his job often required that he "kick the ladder out from under" a project. That meant changing a deadline, budget, or design requirement for the purpose of catalyzing creativity from himself and his teams. We'll learn more from Honda later on.

Where are you operating under assumptions that should be challenged? Gandhi said, "Man is the center of a circle that has no circumference except the limitations he sets upon himself." What artificial or self-imposed limitations contain you? Will you start to challenge them? When?

What if you stop reading right now – put the book down – and create a list of twenty questions related to one of your biggest current challenges? To help get started, you may want to start with "what if..." questions. Remember Einstein's Hour: spend 55 minutes deciding on the questions and 5 minutes answering those questions. Habitually, for most of our lives, we've operated primarily under just the opposite ratio. Isn't it time for a change?

All of us assume the role of teacher from time to time – whether as parents, professionals, sales people, mentors, leaders, or coaches. A few questions a *teacher* might ask:

- What if I had half the budget?
- What if I had half the time?
- If my budget / time / resources were unlimited, what options would I consider?
- What if I had to teach this using a song? ... video?
- What if I had to use a story? ... a poem? ... a metaphor?
- What if I could only use printed materials? ...pictures?
- What if I needed the students to teach each other (or their parents) this lesson?
- What if I had to relate this lesson to a sport, a current event, a famous building, or something in nature?
- What if a cartoon character were teaching this?
- What if I asked the students to teach the lesson before I taught them anything about the topic? What if I did this and involved parents, siblings, grandparents, or other family members?
- Who is a master at engaging my audience – what can I borrow?
- How can I incorporate curiosity? ...humor? ...surprise?
- What if only 20% of my time is highly effective? How can I double that?
- How can I both help people and teach self-sufficiency? (borrowed from Jim Collins' Genius of the "AND")
- How can we feed the hungry today and help them to be able to feed themselves tomorrow?

Collect some questions a *parent* might pursue:

- What simple habit could we easily build into our family routine that would have a significant positive impact?

- What kind of vacation could we take (that would cost nothing / that requires only driving / that will immerse us in history / biology / geography) that my children will remember fondly for the rest of their lives?
- What would inspire the kids to want to do their chores?

Collect some questions a **business leader** might pursue:
- Hiring Talent: how can I get the garden to weed itself?
- If we had no budget, what marketing options could we create? What strategies are free and highly effective?
- If we had to make this 10 year vision a reality in the next 6 months, how could we make that happen?
- Who else reaches our customers that might be a perfect business alliance?
- What small and simple thing can we do to double our number of raving fans?
- How could we make training twice as effective with half the time/budget?
- What is a simple way to keep the vision alive and in front of us on a daily basis?
- What questions can we ask during meetings that dramatically improve engagement/accountability/trust?

Experiment with the questions. Become a collector of questions and then modify them slightly or drastically. Settle on a few that you will pursue.

I recently spoke for one of the most inspiring non-profits I've ever encountered. A member of their leadership team took me back to the airport and we discussed one of his projects, cultivating large donors. He asked how creativity might apply to this project and this is an excerpt of an email I sent to him as a follow up to the conversation.

You were asking about creativity and mentioned something about effectiveness. Please allow some food for thought... Einstein was once asked if he had one hour to solve a difficult problem, how would he do it? His response: "I'd spend the first 55 minutes figuring out what questions to ask and the last 5 minutes asking and answering those questions."

Applying this your world might include asking questions like:

- *How can I get the same results with just seven hours as my average work week? (he currently gives this 70 hours/week)*
- *How can I have 2 or 4 or 10 or 50 people at each one of my very powerful conversations? What group already gets together where I could attend, would have to do none of the inviting, and would produce leveraged (5x, 10x, 100x) results?*
- *Could I make a video that does the work for me, perhaps even getting twice my results in one year for one 2-minute video? Could the video be part of a raving fans appreciation program?*
- *How can I double my results without leaving the office?*
- *How can I enlist a few raving fans to do all of my work so that I'm no longer needed to do it, and the results are better than they currently are?*
- *When I leave a good meeting with someone, could I help them to get three of their friends to make the same commitment?*

In the mid 1980s, Intel was struggling as a company when a conversation between the cofounders of led to this question, as described by Andy Grove. "I turned back to Gordon and I asked, 'If we got kicked out and the board brought in a new CEO, what do you think he would do?' Gordon [Moore] answered without hesitation, 'He would get us out of memories [the memory chip business].' I stared at him, numb, then said, 'Why shouldn't you and I walk out the door, come back and do it ourselves?'" Intel did get out of the memory business, put all their eggs in the basket of processors, and the rest is history!

Chicken Soup for the Soul co-authors explored this question: Mark Victor Hansen asked Jack Canfield how they could sell 1 million copies in a single day.

Great organizations, cultures, families, teachers, leaders pursue great questions. Use questions to change the world. Collect questions. Improve them. Ask them of yourself, your peers, your organization. The quality of our lives – our teaching, our coaching our families, our organizations – hinges on the quality of the questions we pursue. What questions will you pursue?

World-class innovators ask more questions about more things from more angles and with more persistence. Remember, good is the enemy of great!

Expect

His last name was very familiar. It's plastered on buildings across the country that are owned by his family. He had my attention when he told me that he stopped listening to my keynote about a third of the way through. The interaction took place in Seattle. I was signing books after a speech on *"Creative Leadership: Building a Culture of Innovation"* and he bought books for his leadership team. His first words to me were, "Jonathan, I loved your talk…" but then he said, "I have to admit… I stopped listening after you explained the Innovator's Equation." I thought to myself, *"What?"* as I stared at him and tried to smile. In the back of my mind, I was thinking, "Great. Where's this going?"

He continued: "That equation flipped my perspective upside down. It floored me. I realized that we used to run our business with your Innovator's Equation, but for much too long, we've been stuck on six plus four. I wish I could have heard the rest of your talk, but I was fixated on ways to get the organization back to your equation, to get my own thinking back to your equation. I can't tell you how much this means to me... or will mean to our business. Jonathan, thank you!"

It flipped his perspective upside down! That's a typical reaction people have when the really get the Innovator's Equation. It radically alters their paradigm. Some get upset because they realize how profoundly their lives, careers, and societal impact has been limited by the 6 + 4. Every time I speak on this topic, the equation gives me a "frying pan" moment. I continually need to do some serious work in this area. What is this *Innovator's Equation?*

Take a look at the two math problems below.

$$6 + 4 = \underline{\hspace{1cm}}$$

$$\underline{\hspace{0.5cm}} + \underline{\hspace{0.5cm}} = 10$$

How many answers are there to the first problem? Just one. The answer: 10. What about the second problem? There are an infinite number of answers. 1 + 9, 0 + 10, -1 + 11, 0.1 + 9.9, 0.01 + 9.99, etc. I call the bottom scenario the *Innovator's Equation.* For some of you, this is the first math problem you've looked at in over a decade. For others, you are wishing we could put some variables in there and keep going. Some are even ready to debate that the first problem does, indeed, have more than one solution. What's the point? Most of us spend most of our lives and solve most of our problems using the first equation. We have 6 people on our team and a budget of 4, so the result we can create is 10. Real estate comps in the area say 6 and the home we are looking to sell says 4, so our sale price will be 10. Our resume says 6 and the current job market says 4, so the jobs we apply for are 10. Put another way, "Jonathan, if you worked where I work... were married to my spouse... had to deal with my in-laws... lived where I live... had my bank account... then you'd get what I have." Yes, 10. The most creative people and organizations use the second equation, the Innovator's Equation, more frequently and more consistently than the rest of us. They start on the right side of the equation, essentially asking, "What results do we want to create?" It's usually more than 10! They may stay on that side of the equation for a long time before looking at the left side and asking, "What resources do we need to acquire, borrow, develop, etc. in order to get the results we've decided to pursue?"

A powerful example of this approach: for over a decade, Walt Disney did not entertain conversations regarding "How much will Disneyland cost?" He knew that this question would invoke the first equation, $6 + 4 = \_\_$, and follow-up questions like, "Do we have the resources, skillset, or experience to do this?" and "Can we afford that?" Disney wanted all the focus to go towards "What do we want to create?" "What kind of a place do we wish existed?" As the dream became clearer and more compelling, he finally started to ask, "How do we make this a reality?" (What goes on the left side of the equation?) Even Walt's wife, Lillian, worried from the first equation. Walt described it this way, "When I started on Disneyland, my wife used to say, 'But why do you want to build an amusement park? They're so dirty.' I told her that was just the point – mine wouldn't be." The dream of Disneyland grew over the course of about fifteen years. Walt would take his two daughters to Griffith park on Saturdays and sit on a park bench while his girls rode the carousel. When the ride ended, Walt was disappointed to see that some of the horses had chipped and faded paint. Not all of them jumped. Sitting on that bench Saturday after Saturday, Walt would feed and nurture a series of "What if..." questions. What if there were a place "where parents and children could have fun together?" What if our park's carousel had "no chipped paint and all the horses jump?" What if the magic didn't disappear, didn't fade, only grew more incredible? What if?

It began as the smallest seed of an idea, but Walt did something most of us rarely do. He watered, protected, and nurtured that idea. It grew. He expected it to grow. He helped it grow. As it grew, he didn't let others pluck it out of the ground, nor did he pluck it out himself. How often do we let others pluck our seedling ideas out of the ground? How often do we do it ourselves? I'm convinced that most of us dream with that $6 + 4$ mindset. As a result, our dreams are small. If your dreams aren't big enough and bold enough to flood your life with passion, you're living with the wrong equation.

After nurturing these "What if" questions for over a decade, Walt jumped out of bed in the wee hours of the morning with the idea… Perhaps one of the fledgling television networks would help pay for Walt's dream! It took some serious convincing, but one of the networks finally agreed to fund the dream in return for a television series called, "Walt Disney's Disneyland."

About a year after Disneyland opened, Walt saw the Matterhorn while vacationing with his family in Europe. He sent a postcard back to one of his Imagineers with this handwritten message: "Build this!" Growing seeds!

I recently gave a keynote at a gorgeous resort about 90 miles east of Atlanta. The property was on the north shore of Lake Oconee and, while I was there, I had the chance to speak with the man who spearheaded much of the real estate development in the area. He showed me the original plans for the development along with his changes to those plans. His perspective on Lake Oconee could be summed up using the Innovator's Equation. He asked, "How do we make this real estate significantly more valuable (10 or more than 10!)?" "Who would be interested in paying for the project?" He used the Innovator's Equation, decided what he wanted to create, what kind of value, and then worked backwards. Lake Oconee wasn't even a lake until Georgia Power built the Wallace Dam and Hydroelectric Plant on the Oconee River in 1979. The development team asked a series of great questions, including, "How do we create a sustainable energy source and a significant amount of highly desirable real estate?" While most lake development uses a 6 + 4 approach, this development team asked, "How can we create significantly more 'Lakefront' properties?" As a result, they created a unique layout. The road that would typically be lakeside was moved a few hundred yards further away from the lake. Then properties were set aside as common lakefront access with cul-de-sacs feeding from the road. Instead of extremely high value lakefront properties on one side of the road and substantially lower value properties just next door (but merely on the opposite side of the road) this design created about 50% more real estate value and gave everyone in the cul-de-sac communities lakefront access. Different questions with an expectancy that answers existed.

How can we end poverty within 30 years? Mohammad Yunus poses this question. *Pursues* this question. Has the audacity to believe there just may be answers to this question. You'll read more about him in the chapter entitled "End Poverty." Do you think poverty can be eliminated worldwide within 30 years? Yunus didn't think so when he began his work. But, through hundreds of iterated attempts to solve local poverty challenges, he found solutions that are sustainable, duplicatable, and scalable. Experimenting and finding solutions on a small scale fed his expectancy. Through action, Yunus fed his belief, his expectancy that a difference could be made. How often do feed your belief? How could you create "expectancy momentum"?

Do you think it's possible to significantly reduce crime in one of the world's largest, busiest, and most dangerous cities? In 1993, New York City was one of the most crime-infested cities in the world. That was before Bill Bratton took over as Police

Commissioner. Bratton interviewed all the key leaders, and always included one simple question: "We want to reduce crime in New York by 25% within two years. Do you think it's possible?" At NY's highest level of leadership, 5 of 7 leaders answered, "No." Bratton fired those 5. Why? A leader who doesn't think change is possible is not a leader. *How often do you do what you've already decided can't be done?* Of the two remaining leaders who did think it was possible, one described the situation this way: "The car is operating 2 of 8 cylinders. If you get it on 4 cylinders, you can reduce crime by 25%." For over a decade, the NYPD's resources had been focused on maintaining a clean reputation with the community, but not on reducing crime. Members of the NYPD said that rather than trying to prevent crime, they were just cleaning up around it and after it. To iterate an earlier question: "Is the job of police to monitor and respond to crime or to affect and reduce crime... or all of the above?" You may choose to pursue some incredible questions, but, if you've already decided that it can't be done, how likely are you to channel any resources towards accomplishing it? Decide it can't be done and you're not likely to do it. Since Bratton took over, murder and robbery in NY have plummeted by 83%. Over Bratton's first 2 years, crime in NY was reduced by 27%. In the early 1990s, the crime per capita statistics for NY and Chicago were almost identical. Today, Chicago's homicide rate is 6.3 times higher than New York's. 6.3 times higher! Bratton said, "No place is unpoliceable; no crime is immune to better enforcement efforts."

Let's bring this concept of expectancy home. You have challenges that demand creativity. Would your actions convince me that you believe the challenge can be solved? What about your conversations, both verbalized and in your head? Can you double your income this year? Can you take a month vacation every summer without checking in to work at all? Can you 10x your charitable contributions, both in time and money? If you're thinking that you have some work to do in the area of expectancy, you are not alone! To make a difference, you have to believe a difference can be made.

Collect

Become an idea sponge. Many of the innovators highlighted in this book could easily warrant entire books to discover their secrets. Walt Disney is certainly on that list. I will share just a few of my favorite eye-opening Walt Disney lessons within this book. In 1934, Walt decided to create the first full feature length cartoon movie. It would be called Snow White and the Seven Dwarfs. Imagine being part of the team that met with Walt in February of 1934. The Great Depression was raging. Successful companies were dropping like flies. Walt hands you and a few dozen of your peers a few dollars, requesting that you grab a bite to eat and then come back to the studio for a late evening meeting. Upon your return, 50 chairs are arranged around a small wooden makeshift stage with one lightbulb hanging above it. Walt stands under the lightbulb and you join your peers in the audience. Walt Disney himself stands under a swinging light bulb and spins a tale, like only he could. He acts out each part, changing his voice for the evil queen, witch, prince, Show White, and the dwarfs. The one man "show" lasts several *hours*, taking you and the rest of the audience on an emotional roller coaster ride. At its conclusion, Walt announces that this will be the first ever full feature length cartoon. And you are going to make it! For the nearly four years it took to complete Snow White, many of the Disney artists said that Walt's one man show sustained them. The company was almost bankrupt, even mortgaging future revenues from Mickey, Donald, Goofy, and Donald as collateral against loans to keep production going.

How many dwarf names? If you were part of the team and wanted to get things rolling, how many dwarf names would you come up with? The movie will be called *Snow White and the Seven*

Dwarfs. So what does your process look like for selecting dwarf names? I've asked this question to thousands of people and the most common response is, "Come up with 10, 15, or 20 dwarf names. That might take twenty minutes, an hour, perhaps a few hours, or even a few days. Then we'd narrow it down to 7." How? That might be a vote at a meeting on Friday.

For over two years... *TWO YEARS...* the Disney team worked with 64 dwarf names. But it was more than names. They had voices, character traits, personalities, physical attributes, and interactions among variations of the 64 dwarfs. They even brought in actors to portray possible scenes between various dwarf combinations. Imagine this: "Let's put dwarf 1, 17, and 44 in that scene. No! Number 1 doesn't fit. Replace him with 28 and try the scene from the top!" Some of my favorite names and combinations:

Dirty, Hungry, and Weepy
Jumpy, Deafy, and Dumpy
Lazy, Soulful, and Dizzy
Thrifty, Nifty, and Busy

Imagine swapping names around and creating stories that work well with your combination... let's put Deafy and Soulful together for a song or let Weepy and Busy work side by side in the mine! The 64 dwarf options were kept alive for over two years before the team finalized the combination that would star in the first ever full-feature cartoon movie. In the creative process, quantity is a catalyst for quality. Quantity facilitates quality. Quantity of options. How many movies have you seen that were release in 1937? One. Snow White and the Seven Dwarfs. Quantity = Quality. Only here!

Along our spectrum of creativity, I find that people often need a hand making small steps towards becoming more creative. Part of becoming more creative is getting better at connecting dots, even when they are not so obvious. Take a few minutes today to practice connecting dots. How can the 64 dwarfs story apply to your life and work? Can you think of 5 areas of your life where it applies? 10?

I was facilitating a workshop for a major University and I promised the leadership that they may not like me very much by the time we took our first break of the day. Some readers may not be surprised to hear that I succeeded! The University asked me to help them think about education 50 to 100 years in the future. What could they start doing know to prepare? While I don't pretend to know what education – or anything else – will look like 50 to 100 years from now, I certainly believe that a series of "What if" questions can help us to create part of that future. As the brilliant physicist Niels Bohr said, "It is very hard to predict, especially the future."

As a group, we explored some "what if's" and even imagined a Pandora for education model, where a student builds personalized learning channels. For a student who loves baseball and fast-talking teachers, all the video math lessons might include baseball scenarios taught by a New Yorker. I get to speak for many schools and joked with this group that students often tell me that they'd rather learn from a YouTube video than from their teachers. The leadership didn't find this quite as funny as I did. By about 10:30 am, I think our love/hate relationship was well-established! After that first break, I knew it was time to connect dots where some attendees had not seen connection, including this 64 dwarfs example. One leader, who just happened to be the president of the university, bluntly said, "Jonathan, we're not making movies. Quite frankly, I don't see how this relates to our university." I didn't like the way he said it, so I ran and hid in the bathroom. Kidding! Socrates is one of my favorite leaders from history. He said, "I cannot teach anyone anything. I can only make them think." Socrates accomplished this goal by asking questions. Borrowing Socrates' approach, I looked at the executive and asked, "When you have a challenge that might benefit from creativity, how many possible solutions do you usually consider?" He made a face and put his hands up, as if to say, "It depends on the challenge." I continued. "Let's look at a specific example: perhaps *engaging (and retaining!) current students.*"

He replied, "I don't know, maybe we consider six or eight strategies."

I said, "Okay. How long do you weigh these options before taking action?"

He laughed, "We usually decide it at one meeting. Naturally, with the board, it might take a few months before we have that meeting, but I'd say one or two meetings."

I asked, "What part of the 64 dwarf story could apply here?"

He stood up and walked to the front of the group before responding. "I get it. We could come up with a few more options and let them marinate a little longer before finalizing." For a moment, it looked like he might not hate me anymore! An *'Aha!'* expression crossed his face. "We could play around with various combinations of the ideas, as well, like Disney did with dwarf # 1, 17, and 44!" Before he went back to his seat, he stood there shaking his head and softly explained to me, his peers, or maybe just himself, "We decide. We execute. We don't allow more ideas, time for marinating, or playing around with combining ideas. We – the leadership – are a decision-making machine…" His next few words were quiet, but full of conviction and remorse. And everyone nearby heard him: "*…and we're killing creativity!*"

Let's connect some dots in your life. Add a few options to what you might eat for dinner this evening, or how you could spend the weekend. Collect options for ways to teach a success principle to your children or how to show a loved one you appreciate them. Spend a few minutes thinking about 4 or 5 (or maybe even 10 or 20) amazing vacations and then add to that list over the next few weeks. The extra options don't have to be entirely unique. For example, you could plan a family road trip and consider renting an RV, camping, staying with friends you know along the way, one parent flying home to work for a week or two before rejoining the trip, inviting a friend or another family to join you for a segment of the trip, volunteering to help out at a small farm along the journey, etc. Collect ideas on how to make your conversations more interesting or meaningful. Steal strategies from others, shamelessly. Watch great interviewers and take some notes on their tactics. Ask people for their advice in this area. Ask what doesn't work. Become an idea sponge! Collect approaches for building a fun fitness routine or to make a healthy diet more enjoyable. Collect questions so that you can make a point without being the one with all the answers. How often do you send an email without coming up with more than one option for the subject line? Or the number of bullet points? Or the first sentence? Practice creating options. Expand those options. Get ideas and input from more people than you currently do. Remember, you are simply gathering ideas, perspectives, experiences, options.

Combine some of the above ideas. In the "Entrepreneur Adventure" camps that I've run, we have the aspiring entrepreneurs create dozens of ways to make money doing things that they love.

I get it. 64 dwarf names for over 2 years might get you fired. But apply a version of this! Collect more ideas than you typically do, from more sources than you typically do. Let those ideas marinate a little longer than you typically do. Three subject lines for an email instead of one. Let it marinate for 3 minutes instead of hitting send.

5% Iterate!

The ideas you collect won't work for you. How's that for expecting answers? Rephrase that: the ideas you collect might need to be modified by 5%. In workshops, we often refer to this as as "Build-build-build-build-build-jump!" You take an idea and make multiple iterations with only minor changes before jumping to a different idea. Naturally, you can also jump back and forth as you continue to iterate. We'll explore many very practical examples, especially in the "Who wants a Free Boat" chapter.

Sal Khan asked: "Is the job of the teacher to teach or to facilitate learning?" How can we iterate, or 5%, that idea? I played a lot of basketball in my life. In my book, *Who are you BECOMING?*, I share a story of my college team losing a playoff game that we could easily have won. The root cause of our defeat: character. Not skill. Not talent. A few years before that season, when I was fifteen-years-old, my father bought me a book written by one of my favorite NBA players of all time, Larry Bird. I read the book immediately. Reminders or encouragement from my father were unnecessary. On the bottom of page 253, Larry Bird shared a story that captivated me. His high school coach, Jim Jones, told him, "No matter how many shots you take, somewhere there's a kid out there taking one more. If you dribble a million times a day, someone is dribbling a million and one." Larry would be practicing, about to call it a day, and he'd think to himself, "No. Somebody else is still practicing. Somebody – somewhere – is playing that extra ten or fifteen minutes and he's going to beat me someday." Bird would stay on the court, extending his practice time, then think, "Maybe that guy is practicing his free throws now." Bird would then go to the line to work on his free throws. During his NBA career, Bird said, "I still wonder if somebody, somewhere, was practicing more than me." Bird once joked, "I finally met that player in Magic Johnson... He won some and I won some."

I re-read that short paragraph, put a bookmark in the book, and walked out of the house to my driveway basketball court. On that afternoon, from reading that one paragraph, my work ethic in basketball changed forever.

Is the job of the teacher to teach or to facilitate learning?

Is the job of the parent to teach character or to facilitate character development?

Is the job of the leader to inspire or to facilitate inspiration?

Is the job of the leader to hold people accountable or to ensure that accountability exists?

Is the job of the leader to communicate the vision or to make sure that the vision is communicated?

5%. Iterate. Too many leaders (including coaches, teachers, and parents) seem to get confused here. Leaders understand leverage. If you don't understand and use leverage, you don't really understand leadership. My father leveraged a resource to teach me a life lesson. What resources could you leverage?

Basketball coach, Phil Jackson won eleven NBA championships as a coach and two as a player. Thirteen championships! As a coach, each Christmas Jackson would give each of his players a book. The books were personally selected to speak into the recipient's life at that moment. Did Phil Jackson happen to read 12 books each year and think to himself, "Perfect! I'll give this one to Jordan, this to Scottie Pippen, this to Kobe, this to Shaq…"? Not quite. Jackson understood leverage and leadership! He sought tools that could multiply his leadership.

Gifted books ranged from S. E. Hinton's **The Outsiders** (Scottie Pippen) to Sun Tzu's **The Art of War** (Kobe Bryant), Robert Pirsig's **Zen and the Art of Motorcycle Maintenance** (Dennis Rodman) to Herman Hesse's **Siddhartha** (Shaquille O'Neal), Toni Morrison's **Song of Solomon** (Michael Jordan) to Harold Moore and Joseph Galloway's **We Were Soldiers Once… And Young** (Luke Walton, whose father, Bill, played for a coach you'll read about later in the book, John Wooden). Each book was gifted with that particular player in mind. Can you imagine selecting the books for Dennis Rodman? Just a few years ago, Phil Jackson gave each of the N.Y. Knicks a copy of Sam Smith's **There Is No Next**, about the dominant legacy of Michael Jordan. Jackson hoped that the players, especially the Knicks biggest scorer at the time, Carmelo Anthony, would grasp the level of intensity needed to be a champion.

Take an idea, a question, an option, and iterate it. The most creative people in history tend to wonder, "How would that look if...?"

Crash and Live...so you can Learn – F^4(OB)

You need to fail more. And you know it. Fail. But fail fast, forward, frequently, and, when possible, off Broadway. F^4(OB). Fail Forward Fast Frequently (Off Broadway). Iterate. Experiment. Try things. Lots of things. But learn from them. Fail. Mess up. But pay attention to the lessons. Pull the lessons out of each attempt. Crash early and often, but survive the crashes so you can learn from them and try again.

Amazon founder, Jeff Bezos, said, "It's not an experiment if you know it's going to work." This final pillar is the lid on creativity for most of us. We allow this one to stop us. I certainly do. How and Why? My father-in-law retired recently. We joke that he needed to retire to get caught up on soccer! The soccer season around the world seems to never end. One cup is starting, another ending, and the big one is right around the corner! Which big one? The World Cup? Copa America? Euro Cup? Champions League Cup? I thought there was just a World Cup. Wow, was I wrong! Not sure you can ever get caught up on soccer!

Soccer is a game of moments. I find this to be one of the most intriguing aspects of the game. They play an intensely physical 90 minutes of soccer and score, at least in the 2022 World Cup, an average of 2.7 total goals per game. Those goals are scored in a moment. Losing focus or letting fatigue affect you can easily lead to the difference between winning and losing. It is truly a game of moments. In that sense, soccer is a great metaphor for life. How often do we say something or make a simple gesture in the moment that either invites creativity or dismisses it, that either encourages or discourages? In the moments, we also allow our thoughts to follow a positive "What if..." or a negative "What if... (it goes wrong/this idea fails/they don't like the idea)" With the low scoring, about 1 out of 4 of World Cup soccer games end regulation in a tie score. In later rounds of the tournament, the victor will be decided by overtime and, if necessary, penalty kicks (PK). 75% of penalty kicks in professional soccer end in the goal. Why? Imagine lining up as the goalkeeper trying to stop a penalty kick. The ball is kicked 70+ mph and reaches the goal line in 1/3 of a second. The goal is 24 feet wide and 8 feet high. What does the goalkeeper do? Guess. Anticipate, which is a fancy word for making an educated guess. On 57% of PKs, goalkeepers anticipate and leap to the kicker's strong side. Much like pulling the ball in baseball, for a right footed kicker, the strong side is the left side of the goal. Kickers have more power to their strong side. On 41% of PKs, goalkeepers guess towards the kicker's weak side. Wait! We're missing something. What happens with that last 2%? Maybe you've guessed (or anticipated) the answer. On 2% of the PKs, goalkeepers stay where they are, anticipating that the kicker will fire the ball right down the middle. If kickers score 75% of the time, but the goalkeeper only stays in the middle 2% of the time, wouldn't a ball kicked straight down the middle go into the net 98% of the time? Of course, this assumes that the goalkeepers don't adjust their educated guesses. Why would you not kick the ball right down the middle? Imagine that Lionel Messi, the highest paid soccer player in the world, lines up for a PK in one of the biggest games of his life. He decides to "get creative" and kick the ball right down the middle. It just so happens that the goalkeeper makes that 2% decision to stay right at home. The ball is struck with force and in 1/3 of a second, the goalkeeper is holding Messi's ball and wearing a gigantic smile. The World Cup is over and Messi is not allowed back into his home country, Argentina!

What were you thinking, Messi? How could you do that, Messi? I could have kicked the ball right down the middle, Messi. We just might have a Messi jersey bonfire after that creative failure.

What is the most consistent lid on our creativity? The chance that it might not work out. The possibility of failure. The fear of hearing, even if only from ourselves, that refrain, "What were you thinking?" Messi can kick it to one side or the other and score at a higher rate than most. If the goalkeeper anticipates correctly and makes a great play, at least Messi can go home looking like he gave it his all. He knows the likelihood of failure and success. It's the same reason very few adults give the advice, "Skip college and start a business." After a recent keynote in San Diego, one attendee told me that her daughter opted out of college. Instead, they invested ~$20,000 in helping her start a photography business and she's making more than most college grads less than 2 years into the venture. Mom explained to me that the lessons her daughter has learned are worth even more than the financial return. But what if that didn't go so well? That's a thought most of us entertain, perhaps all too often.

We spend significant time on the wrong "What if..." question. What if it doesn't work? F4(OB) challenges us to find ways to try things that might not work. Change the question. What are some ways to experiment that don't cost your entire life's savings, but might provide valuable feedback? Before you write an entire book write a 1 page article. Get feedback from the real world on that article. Then re-write it or write a 2nd article. As a parent, before you announce the new chores process, try it for one day. Try an hour on Sunday without technology before announcing that every weekend will be technology-free. A friend of mine owns a successful craft brewery. Before he bought any equipment, he visited 60 craft breweries across the country, absorbing a massive amount of both lessons and warnings from their experiences. Then he started very small with used equipment and only selling locally on tap before scaling up. His F4(OB) included studying failures of others. How's that for off-broadway… learning from failures that don't cost you too much? Try things that might not work before you are on the world's stage, things that won't cost you your job or home. Read the chapter on the Wright Brothers. Their story was a wake-up call for me on the power of learning from failure without dying!

This is your framework. You do it well… sometimes. Most of us are incredibly creative in moments and pockets. Moments of our lives and pockets of our lives. There are areas of your life with incredible potential. It took decades for us to "unlearn creative behavior." Will you be intentional about unleashing creativity into your world?

The rest of the book will give you example after example of creativity unleashed in all walks of life. Pick any chapter and begin. Ponder how that scenario might be similar to one you face. Question the strategies of the people you meet in each chapter. Let their stories inspire, encourage, and challenge you.

Here's to the Crazy Ones!

If you want to find out if someone can lead, there is a simple test. It works every time. Ask that person to make a positive change. That's it. Leaders change things. Good leaders change things for the better.

When Steve Jobs came back to Apple after a 12 year "vacation", he initiated two game changers almost immediately. First, he cut the product line by 70%. This move allowed for a tremendous focus. It eliminated significant distractions and freed up resources for that focus. About a decade later, Jobs received a phone call from a new CEO for another iconic brand that needed to change things. In 2006, Mark Parker had just take over the reins at Nike and was seeking advice. Jobs' advice was simple. He told Parker that Nike makes some incredible products, some of the most sought-after sneakers and sports apparel in the world. And Nike makes some 'crap'. Parker thought Jobs would laugh after making that statement, but he didn't. Jobs continued by challenging Nike to stop making the 'crap' and focus all of Nike's energy on incredible products. Change focus.

Jobs' second game changer was a commercial that clearly communicated Apple's identity to the world and, perhaps more importantly at that moment in time, to its own employees. You've probably seen the commercial. In the longer version, 17 creative icons from the 20th century are projected in black and white.

The creative legends included Albert Einstein, Bob Dylan, Martin Luther King, Jr., Richard Branson, John Lennon, Buckminster Fuller, Thomas Edison, Mohandas Gandhi, Amelia Earhart, Alfred Hitchcock, Frank Lloyd Wright and Pablo Picasso.

Jobs would often reiterate: "Picasso had a saying. 'Good artists copy, great artists steal.' And we have always been shameless about stealing great ideas."

In the commercial, we hear a narrator (Richard Dreyfuss or Steve Jobs, himself) paint a picture of creativity and leadership:

Here's to the crazy ones.
The misfits.
The rebels.
The troublemakers.
The round pegs in the square holes.
The ones who see things differently.
They're not fond of rules.
And they have no respect for the status quo.
You can quote them, disagree with them,
glorify or vilify them.
About the only thing you can't do is ignore them.
Because they change things.
They push the human race forward.
While some may see them as the crazy ones,
we see genius.
Because the people who are crazy enough to think
they can change the world, are the ones who do.

They change things! Let that phrase affect you. Creative leaders see something that needs to be changed and they set out to change it. They change a relationship, change a conversation, change a habit, change a mindset, change their approach to communication...

About the only thing you can't do is ignore them.
Because they change things.
... they CHANGE things...
*... they **CHANGE** things...*

Throughout this book, we'll explore some captivating lessons from several of the stars of this commercial as well as many other world-class innovators. Each one has something to teach us.

Napoleon Hill, author of one of the 20th Century's great books on success entitled **Think and Grow Rich**, once asked Thomas Edison if he ever tired of being asked about all the failures in his experiments to invent a working light bulb. Edison's reply challenged Hill and certainly challenges me. To paraphrase Edison:

"I knew that I would eventually run out of ways that didn't work. If I had not found a solution, I'd be still in the lab right now, instead of standing here, talking with you."

Two beautiful parts to that answer. 1) Edison was crossing things off the list. That didn't work. Next! 2) Edison asked until he uncovered answers. Sought until he found. Knocked until a door opened.

Edison was even creative in his energy management. He took short naps in his laboratory throughout the day. How many of us just keep working, even when our energy is extremely low and we're getting just about nothing accomplished?

Buckminster Fuller put it this way: "Everyone is born a genius, but the process of living de-geniuses them."

So often, we get caught up in thinking we need to change some big things. Figuring out what those big things are can paralyze us. Sometimes, we need to step back and simply decide to make something better. To change something. It could be a little thing. One habit. How you initiate conversations with your spouse or a co-worker. Your tone of voice when answering the phone. Something as simple as the facial expression when you greet a colleague, friend or family member. How you begin or end your day. The way you motivate yourself to eat healthy or exercise regularly. What kinds of books you surround yourself with and how often you open them. What quotes, ideas, or questions you reflect on most.

They CHANGE thing! Let this phrase sink in. Let it affect you.

THEY CHANGE THINGS!

End Poverty... (in 30 Years?)

How can we end poverty globally within 30 years? If we're honest, most of us probably think, "Not a chance!" This question drives the heart and soul of Nobel Peace Prize winner, Muhammad Yunus, whose life is a testament to the pursuit of great questions. But it's more than that. Yunus started where he was and slowly built both bigger questions and a belief that those questions had answers. In his own words, "We prepare our students for jobs and careers, but we don't teach them to think as individuals about what kind of world they would create."

Within 30 years, Yunus would like poverty to only exist in museums. To have that kind of dramatic impact, he sought self-sustainable and scalable vehicles, and it's working. But – and this is a big but – he didn't think that big in the beginning. In fact, he slowly built a belief – an expectancy – that he could help a handful of people get out of poverty. That expectancy, like a tiny seed, didn't grow into a global scale belief overnight.

Muhammad Yunus pursued different questions when he began the Grameen (*"Village"*) Bank for the poor. He wasn't a banker, so he didn't see with their lenses. In fact, Yunus says that the consistent temptation is to see everything through "profit-maximizing" lenses, instead of "poverty-ending" or "make the world better" lenses. A traditional banker told Yunus that he had flipped the banking world upside down. Yunus replied that the banking industry had been standing on its head, so he had simply flipped it over so it could now stand on its feet. Grameen looked at the approach of most traditional banks and did the opposite.

Let's compare (TB=Traditional Bank, GB=Grameen Bank):

TB: "Are the poor credit-worthy?"

GB: "Are the banks people-worthy?"

TB: Collateral required

35

GB: No collateral required
TB: Lend to rich
GB: Lend to poor
TB: Go to the cities
GB: Go to the small villages
TB: Lawyers and big law firms involved
GB: Not a single lawyer
TB: Lend to men
GB: Lend to women (97% of all borrowers)
TB: Owned by rich
GB: Owned by poor (95% owned by borrowers)
TB: Interested in past of their borrowers to determine lending
GB: Interested primarily in the future of their borrowers
TB: Purpose is maximizing profit
GB: Purpose is ending poverty
TB: Few people are entrepreneurial
GB: All people are entrepreneurial – encourage it
TB: Beggars need hand-outs and charity
GB: Beggars are worthy of loans and will repay those loans
TB: When repayment is delayed, it's the fault of the borrower
GB: When repayment is delayed, look at the system and consider restructuring the loan to better fit the borrower

Could this really work? Of course, these statements are not the way all banks see the world, but some of Grameen's ideas sound more than just a bit unrealistic!

Let the Results Speak! (Not a bad start!)

Over 2,500 branches in Bangladesh

Lends money to over 8 million people, 97% women, in over 40 countries, including 78,000 villages across Bangladesh

Staff of about 27,000

Grameen housing loans have been used by the poorest people in Bangladesh to construct over 650,000 houses (by 2007, update #)
Lends roughly $100 million/month
Average loan $200
98% repayment
Over 100,000 beggars on program, over 20,000 have quit begging as a result of the program, Most beggars are now on their 2nd and 3rd loans
Over 50,000 school loans...

Humble Beginnings: $27 and a Desire to Serve

How did all this get started? I often find myself in conversations with people who describe a feeling that they should be doing something more, something bigger, supporting some significant cause. I usually respond by simply saying, "Why not begin where you are?" Most creative legends start out small, affecting something that is practically in their back yard.

In 1974, Yunus was teaching Economics at a university in Bangladesh when he became more aware of the extreme poverty surrounding him. He thought, "Someone needs to help these people. Maybe I could do something?" He spoke to some of the poor people that he passed by on the streets every day and pondered concrete ways that he might be able to help. Mother Teresa once said, "Today it is fashionable to talk about the poor. Unfortunately, it is not fashionable to talk with them." Yunus walked and talked with those in need. A woman named Sufiya told him that she made wicker chairs for a living and was unable to afford wicker, so she borrowed money from a street loan shark. The loan shark charged very high interest, 10% weekly, and required her to sell everything she created to the shark at a price set by the shark. This chair-maker found herself in a perpetual cycle of borrowing to buy wicker, then selling her chairs for a price that was well below market value, then borrowing to buy more wicker. Yunus loaned Sufiya 22 cents to buy enough wicker for one chair, which she sold at fair market value and garnered enough profit to buy wicker for the next chair. The vicious cycle ended for Sufiya and her family with the repayment of a 22 cent loan.

Conversation after conversation exposed similar circumstances. Yunus tallied up the amount of money required to get a group of 42 people out of perpetual poverty. Twenty-seven dollars. Yes, $27. Adjusted to 2023, this would amount to roughly $165. Total. To help 42 people leave the cycle of poverty. Yunus visited a local bank and asked if they would lend the $27 to this small group. The bank's answer was a clear and simple "No!" Yunus said, "I went to the bank and proposed that they lend money to the poor people. The bankers almost fell over."

He had options and a decision to make. He could walk away from the idea, approach other banks, or lend the money out of his own pocket. He ended up lending 42 people a combined total of $27. They all paid him back and it set this group of people on a different path. Yunus could also have given them the money, but said, "When we want to help the poor, we usually offer them charity. Most often we use charity to avoid recognizing the problem and finding the solution for it. Charity becomes a way to shrug off our responsibility. But charity is no solution to poverty. Charity only perpetuates poverty by taking the initiative away from the poor. Charity allows us to go ahead with our own lives without worrying about the lives of the poor. Charity appeases our consciences."

Every dollar of those initial loans was paid back to Yunus. He repeated the process. And repeated the process. And repeated the process. And... You get the picture. Yunus also continued to approach traditional banks, but they continued to turn his proposals down, despite his increasing body of evidence that the poor were repaying these micro-loans and the impact on human life was substantial.

It took 9 years before he was able to convince the Bangladesh government, in 1983, to allow him to officially launch Grameen Bank with this unique approach to lending, now known as micro-lending.

Selena is a Grameen borrower in Bangladesh. In the first of her weekly meetings with a loan officer and group of peers, she was asked, "What did you do with the money?" A requirement for her loan was simply that the money be used to create money-making opportunities. Selena said, "I bought a rickshaw." The loan officer asked, "Does it make you enough money to pay your loan?" She responded, "Yes it makes me two or three dollars every day." Ten years after that first loan, she owned a cow, 2 rice fields, and a three-room house. She had successfully paid off several Grameen loans and, when asked about her dreams for the future, she gleamed. "Our daughter would like to go to school and become a doctor." Selena's whole being communicated that she now knew that this was truly possible! Contagious expectancy in action!

Struggling Members

With a belief that all human beings have entrepreneurial potential, Yunus decided to set up a loan program specifically for beggars. First, a team from Grameen went to the villages to converse with beggars and to listen to their stories. Then, they set up version 1.0 of a "struggling members" loan program. Most of the beggars borrowed about $12 or $15 and paid it back over about a year. The second loan was typically bigger. Over 110,000 beggars have participated in Grameen loan programs. Most of these borrowers are on their second or third loans. In speaking with beggars, the Grameen team asked if they would be interested in bringing an item or two with them that they could sell instead of just asking for money. The idea was explained as being very simple and only a slight change of their current strategy. The beggars were already approaching people, so instead of asking for a hand out, they would have boxes of cookies, candies, or children's toys for sale. It sounded simple enough and realistic. Many beggars were interested, so Grameen tested a loan program with no interest and no timeframe. Yunus challenged the assumptions that very few human beings are entrepreneurs and the economy hinges on that small group creating jobs for the rest. The beggars didn't need sales training. Tens of thousands of "struggling members" have already "graduated" from the program and no longer beg for a living.

Critics and Naysayers

A traditional banker once approached Yunus and suggested that the bank should be renamed "Grameen Women's Bank", since borrowers were primarily women. Yunus thought about the suggestion and then responded that he would change the name, provided the banker change the name of his bank to "Such and Such Men's Bank", since their borrowers were virtually all men. Neither bank name was changed. Grameen's original plan was to lend to 50% men and 50% women, but they quickly found out that their female borrowers consistently created a more significant ripple effect on their families and villages. More of their financial progress went towards their family and the education of their children. After discovering this, Grameen decided to lend primarily to women. Poverty-ending lenses, not profit-maximizing lenses.

Criticism came regularly and rapidly:
- *"The people you are serving must not really be poor. Otherwise, how can they afford to repay their loans?"*
- *"Can't work! It won't be scalable. It might have worked in one village, but it won't work here..."*
- *"This is babysitting, not banking. You and your students [when he was still teaching at the University] are so deeply involved with the clients." (Yunus said that he didn't see how this was such a bad thing.)*

- *"Poor people can't write, so they wouldn't be able to fill out their paperwork."*
- *"They have no collateral."*
- *"They have no money or financial skills."*
- *"Your pay back is good because you're lending to people who aren't truly that poor."*
- *"Your bank is too unconventional. You don't have proper internal controls. You don't have financial benchmarks, auditing procedures."*
- *"Eventually your staff will begin cheating you."*
- *"The problem is that you are professor, not a banker."*

I love Yunus' perspective in relation to many of these criticisms: "Yes, I was a professor, not a banker – which is why I'd spent years trying to convince real bankers to take over my business! …. I have come to see that my innocence about banking helped me a lot. The fact that I was not a trained banker and in fact had never even taken a course on bank operations meant that I was free to think about the process of lending and borrowing without preconceptions. [Otherwise] I would have started with the banking system as it existed and then tried to figure out how the poor could be fitted into that system."

In what other industries, fields, concepts, and parts of life would this approach be worth pursuing? In a sense, you could say this is similar to asking someone who has never been a parent to create parenting strategies, one who has never taught to build a school, one who has never been in government to govern, one who has never mowed a lawn to start a lawn care company.

How does it work?

Grameen borrowers typically begin with a very small loan of about $35. The recipient often trembles, finding it hard to believe that someone trusts her with this much money.

Grameen's repayment rate around the world is world-class, at 98%. When borrowers are asked, "Why do you repay your loan?" their most common answer is "I would feel terrible to let down the other members of my group." Borrowers are put into a small group of peers from the day they request their first loan. Members of that group commit to getting together every single week for one hour. In that meeting, cash payments are collected in person. Each borrower describes what the loan was used for and how that money-making opportunity is working. If someone doesn't show up, the peer group will discuss ways to reach out to that person. Each small group has about 5 people and cannot have more than two closely-related people. Sometimes, group meetings will be used to discuss business topics, including marketing, pricing, seasonality, business cycles, negotiating, customer relations, inventory, or hiring.

If a new borrower asks Grameen staff members, "What would be a good business idea for me?" The standard Grameen response is, "I am sorry, but I'm not smart enough to give you a good business idea. Grameen has lots of money but no business ideas. That's why Grameen has come to you. You have the idea, we have the money. If Grameen had good business ideas, instead of giving the money to you, it would use the money itself to make more money."

Grameen's loan products are all simple interest and most borrowers pay about 2% of their principal each week. For a $200 loan, the weekly payments might be about $4. Total interest never exceeds the original principal. Loan duration and size can vary. Individual branches are designed to be self-sufficient from opening day. Many loans require that a portion of the loan be immediately transferred into the borrower's Grameen saving account. Since payments are made weekly and in person, borrowers who struggle with repayment are flagged very quickly. Yunus says, "Grameen bank has always believed that if the borrower gets into trouble and cannot pay back her loan, it is our responsibility to help her."

Grameen branches also collect deposits from non-Grameen members to help with self-funding and resilience. New branches today are expected to be self-funding and self-sufficient from day one. Scalability. "Poverty-ending" lenses.

Build Operate Transfer – B.O.T. Grameen sets up a microcredit branch in a region where it's desperately needed. They build and operate that branch until it's sustainable, then transfer ownership and management to local people – to the poor. Build, operate, transfer. As a result, branches around the globe are primarily owned and operated by the local poor.

Grameen has provided over 50,000 school loans and students are encouraged to become job-creators, not job-takers. They are consistently told, "Your mothers own a big bank, so create a business idea and bring it to Grameen!"

Opening Branch in Queens, New York

"Are you with the mafia?" In Queens, NY, an early employee of Grameen America heard this when explaining to a potential borrower that the organization made short-term loans at very reasonable interest rates and that he would come around every week to collect payments in cash. When one Queens woman asked, "What happens if someone struggles to make a payment?" he casually responded, "It's no problem. We have a lot of ways to help you and motivate you!"

One of the Queens branch early borrowers was a hair dresser with 8 kids. She ran her business out of a cramped apartment and used part of the first loan to make business cards. Over time, and the course of several successful loans, she rented her own space for the growing business.

Grameen America currently operates in 7 states, with branches in New York, Massachusetts, North Carolina, Nebraska, California, Indiana, Texas, and Puerto Rico. Business loans are 6 to 12 months at 7.5% interest, simple not compounding.

A Few Success Stories!

A quick glance at few success stories touches the possibilities:

Maria (Oakland, CA) combined family recipes for homemade Mexican cheeses and a $1,500 Grameen loan to purchase larger equipment and refrigeration to scale her business.

Nancy (Indianapolis, IN) is a 22-year-old artist who sells her 'Repujado' style art to local restaurants, churches, and individuals. A Grameen loan helped her purchase more art supplies and increase her marketing efforts.

Angeline (Philippines) typically puts in 15-hour days in her variety store, supplying locals with much needed items from milk to medicine. Her first Grameen loan was used to purchase a freezer and added fresh meats and vegetables to her inventory. She now runs the largest variety store in her neighborhood.

Juan and Maria (Columbia) are coffee farmers and combined solutions from several Grameen branches to decide on appropriate fertilizers, install and maintain beetle traps, purchase machinery, and sell their coffee through a cooperative in order to get more consistent pricing and demand.

Anne (Kenya) bought a cow, some poultry, and built a cow shed with her first loan. Before the loan, purchasing milk for the family was out of reach. Anne is a widow who now sells milk, chickens, and eggs to support her family, pay for her three children's schooling, adopt her nephew, and invest in additional livestock.

Other Social Businesses

"A charity dollar has only one life. You use it, it's done. But a social business dollar has endless lives." ~ Muhammad Yunus

Muhammad Yunus, at the time of this writing, is 82 years old. It doesn't appear that he's slowed down in any area of his life. Much of his current work is on the broader topic of "Social Business." He likes to describe three types of organizations: a for-profit business, a not-for-profit business, and a social business. The first exists to generate profit. The second exists to solve a social cause and requires funding, in the form government aid, donations, grants, etc. The third type, the Social Business, exists to solve a social challenge and is completely self-sustaining. It does not require outside funding for continued operation. As a result, it is a scalable solution. Grameen Bank is just one example of such a Social Business. The bank exists to end poverty, using deposits and loans to create a sustainable and scalable business model that does not depend on government or private charity. Much like a McDonald's franchise, the model works and can be replicated throughout the world. Let's briefly look at a few of the *over 100* Social Businesses that Yunus has helped to launch.

Yunus often repeats, "Whenever I see a problem, I immediately go and create a company. We don't have to wait for the government to do it. We can solve our problems.... Human creativity has no limit. It's only a question of how we apply it."

Nutrient-rich Yogurt

Grameen Danone Foods Ltd. (GDFL) was launched in 2006 as a partnership between the global yogurt giant, Danone, and Grameen. GDFL's purpose: Provide poor children with the nutrients often missing from their diets via a yogurt that is made and delivered via a self-sustaining social business. Cups of yogurt are sold for about $0.06 to $0.10 and contain 30% of the recommended daily nutritional value for a growing child. Sales jobs are also given to the poor, who can earn a 10% to 20% commission.

About half of all Bangladeshi children under the age of 5 suffer from moderate to severe malnutrition. When the first Grameen

Danone yogurt product was introduced, most of Bangladesh's poor were also poorly educated about nutrition. Extensive marketing, sales, and educational efforts were introduced to help potential customers understand the value of eating this healthy yogurt. Sales in cups per day rose steadily, averaging 3,500 in 2007 and surpassing 95,000 cups per day by 2010. Has everything been peaches and cream yogurt? Of course not. Obstacles have been similar to those faced by most businesses, including lack of consistent refrigeration, affordably reaching and educating a new market segment, plastic cup cost and recycling, changes in demand (and pricing) for sugar, molasses, and packaging.

Healthcare

Grameen Healthcare (GH) now operates over 60 clinics, a microinsurance program, and an eye hospital. The eye hospital serves patients on a sliding fee scale.

Mobile Phones

Grameenphone is the largest mobile phone operator in Bangladesh, providing cell phone services for over 50 million users within a social business model. In its early phases, sales people would own a phone and allow the poor to make phone calls for a very modest fee, a few pennies per minute.

Water

Much of the accessible drinking water in Bangladesh is contaminated with arsenic. Grameen Healthcare Services and Veolia Water joined forces to create a social business (Grameen Veolia Water) to solve this challenge. The partnership exists to bring safe water to the poor in a sustainable manner. They build and operate water treatment plants and sell higher end bottled water in the cities to help make the business model financially sound.

Sneakers

Grameen partnered with Adidas to create a $2 sneaker that the poor could afford. They created a sneaker that customers would choose to purchase and that did not need to be subsidized, as this would limit the scalability and sustainability of the project. Style, comfort, and product quality matter.

Power and Energy

Grameen Shakti has installed solar power systems for over a half million homes and energy efficient stoves for over 100,000 families.

Dietary Supplements and Malaria Prevention

BASF Grameen was formed to produce and distribute dietary supplements in the form of micronutrient sachets to sprinkle on food as well as mosquito nets to prevent malaria.

Software and Apps

Grameen Intel Social Business (GISB) creates applications to address social challenges including prenatal care, crop yield, soil testing, and fertilizer analysis. Products also include the apps gDraw, to teach drawing skills, and gSlate, to teach basic language skills in Arabic, English, and Bangla.

As a quick side note, Muhammad Yunus does not own a single share in any of the Grameen companies. Build, Operate, Transfer.

Social Business is not a new concept. I see it as the way most successful businesses have been started throughout history. What is a legitimate need of society? And how can we fulfill it in a sustainable manner? What Yunus calls a social business just has a lot more clarity and discipline around that business's priorities. It might be as simple as saying priority one for some businesses is profit maximization. For a social business, priority one is clearly and consistently supporting the social cause in a sustainable and scalable manner. Priority one clearly requires the business to say no to a lot of options, but, as a mentor of mine years ago liked to challenge, "If you're not compelled to say no to a great many things, you lack clarity!"

A recent USA Today article "Monks who make world's best beer have a message" described one business that lives its priorities.

"Inside the sanctuary of the Abbey of St. Sixtus of Westvleteren is a beer lover's dream and a businessman's nightmare. Piety, not profit, is what these monks seek. The St. Sixtus monks break every rule in Business 101 except attention to quality. And therein may lie the secret of their success in brewing a beer that some rank among the world's best and that is so hard to get there's a black market for it."

When RateBeer.com ranked a St. Sixtus brew as the #1 beer in the world, RateBeer.com's director, Joe Tucker, received a call from St. Sixtus. The # 1 ranking had increased demand and the monks were *not* happy. They had no intention to increase production. According to Tucker, "Beer's usually a business; there's a market for it, but the monks don't see it that way." The Father Abbot at St. Sixtus Trappist Abbey says, "We are no brewers. We are monks. We brew beer to be able to afford to be monks."

I can imagine Muhammad Yunus saying, "We are not bankers. We are champions of the poor. We bank to be able to end poverty." Clarity around a purpose. Purpose-maximizing glasses instead of profit-maximizing glasses. With clarity, you will be compelled to say no to a great many things!

In 1919, the Dodge Brothers sued Henry Ford on the grounds that a company should act in the interests of its shareholders ("fiduciary duty") and not for the good of society, its customers or its employees. At the time, the Dodge Brothers were minor shareholders in Ford Motor Company and were seeking an increase in dividends. Henry Ford argued that he preferred to use the corporation's money to build cheaper, better cars and to pay better wages. Ford lost the case in the Michigan Supreme Court. Cornell Law professor, Lynn Stout, wrote an article for the New York Times entitled, "Corporations Don't Have to Maximize Profits" and she builds a simple case that corporations can be formed for any purpose, including solving a social cause. Yunus said, "The challenge I set before anyone who condemns private-sector business is this: If you are a socially conscious person, why don't you run your business in a way that will help achieve social objectives?" Be honest: why do you really do the work that you choose to do? Is it purely to maximize profits?

Clarity in Yunus' words: "Grameen is a tool for reshaping lives, and we never lose sight of that reality." Changing priorities – changing the questions we pursue – changes everything.

Where do you go from here?

How many of the world's challenges could you and I solve if we just looked in our backyards with a different set of glasses? As part of a local church group, I help cook breakfast for the hungry. While writing this chapter, I was at one of the breakfast events that set the current local record for feeding the most people. I couldn't help but think, "Are we succeeding or failing?" Yunus might say that we are succeeding in pursuit of the wrong question. What if we changed the question from: "How can we feed more people?" to "How can we help in such a way that no one in our local community needs to be fed?" Yunus might ask, "Are you feeding them to help them or to feel like you are helping them?" I thought about this as I flipped pancakes. Maybe we can serve food for the next several months, but simultaneously talk with – and strengthen relationships with – those being fed. At some point, we could invite the hungry into the kitchen to help with the meal preparation. Some are likely already very capable cooks. Others might need some instruction. Perhaps this kitchen could then make more food than is required by this group and they could sell breakfast sandwiches to go or for delivery to local businesses or schools. To be sure, there are many ways to go forward with this, but just imagine how the pursuit of better questions opens the door to better solutions.

Simple. As Yunus says, "Things are never as complicated as they seem. It is only our arrogance that prompts us to find unnecessarily complicated answers to simple problems."

Paul Zane Pilzer (former NYU professor, author of eleven books, and economics advisor to several U.S. presidents) brings an interesting perspective. Pilzer says that most economics textbooks start with a drastically incorrect assumption. The texts essentially define economics as the study of how people make choices under conditions of scarcity. In other words, "There's a pie here, and economics is how you cut it up to determine who gets what." This assumption has consequences. Pilzer essentially declares, "Throw away the knife and let's just bake a bigger pie.'" Several of Pilzer's books explain in depth that resources are not necessarily scarce or limited. Maybe the easiest way to understand this: many of the biggest companies in the world produce and sell things that did not even exist in a few years or decades ago. Cell phones. Software. Music. Ideas. Entertainment. Experiences. Education. Training. In a way, I believe that Yunus' idea of social business has the ability to help us reframe our perspective not only on the size of the pie that we can create, but what kind of a pie, how many pies, and who will help create those pies.

Allow these words of Muhammad Yunus to challenge you!

"My greatest challenge has been to change the mindset of people. Mindsets play strange tricks on us. We see things the way our minds have instructed our eyes to see."

"Poor people are like bonsai trees. When you plant the best seed from the tallest tree in a tiny flowerpot, you get a replica of the tallest tree, only inches tall."

"Once poverty is gone, we'll need to build museums to display its horrors to future generations. They'll wonder why poverty continued so long in human society."

Kindergarten SuperTeacher!

Twenty-one children sat spell-bound. They were intrigued... and quiet. They danced, raised their hands to answer questions, knew the correct answers almost every time, made shapes with their arms, legs, or entire bodies. Make no mistake, every child in the classroom was learning. Not just learning, but learning quickly, retaining the information, and enjoying the process. Did they need course correction? Of course. But it came in very subtle, yet highly effective and quick bursts. Some course correction came in the form of song, a poetic phrase, or a light-hearted humorous statement. The children seemed to be used to this and responded very well.

I had to know some of the thinking behind this magic. What was behind the curtain? In that teacher's own words, this is the magic.

When I became a teacher, I knew that I wanted my classroom environment and lessons to be different. I wanted to steer as far away from the traditional textbook and pencil norm as possible. I have been teaching first grade for the past 6 years. I have come to learn through experience what the key necessities are to keep this age group focused, interested and motivated to learn. At the beginning of each lesson my goal is to hook the children in and make the lessons for each day meaningful and purposeful to the kids. If the children don't understand the reason for learning the content, they lack in motivation. I always try to think of songs and jingles to assist the class with recalling specific facts. Movements are key as well. If the children go home and say 'my teacher was jumping and skipping around the room' they are 100% correct. My goal is to make a lasting impression each day. Small group work, games, dances... whatever it takes to make learning fun is my motto.

Intriguing! As with every lesson in this book, this one can be applied to so many areas of our lives:

- Dinner time with the family
- Toasting special occasions (Holiday, wedding, etc.)
- Facilitating a meeting (or simply making a point in a meeting)
- Emails
- Coaching a sport

Let's dissect Mrs. Caldas' approach. Some questions she asks:

- What is the meaning, the purpose, the "Why?"
- What are the key necessities to maintain this group's focus, interest and motivation?
- How can I hook the kids in the beginning of the lesson?
- What will keep listeners focused, motivated, interested?
- What might assist with recall?
- How can we incorporate movement and make it fun?
- How can each day leave a lasting impression?

It was a start, but I wanted to understand more. Mrs. Caldas' explanation certainly aligned with what I had witnessed in the classroom. There was a rhythm to her teaching. She wove in curiosity and engaged every single child. I watched her call on a child in such a way that it brought the child's attention back without creating an uncomfortable moment. She looked at Ryan, said his name with an upbeat tone, and then continued, "Ryan, we were just talking about the weather, right?" A nod from Ryan, who wasn't paying much attention just moments ago. Mrs. Caldas maintained eye contact and walked towards Ryan and used exaggerated hand gestures as she continued, "What if, Ryan, we had sunny days every single day for the rest of this week? Would you like that?" Ryan nods his head. "Ryan, why would you like that?"

Ryan responded, "Outdoor recess! Oh, and I have soccer. It's not so fun in the rain. Well, it's actually really, really fun in the rain, but sometimes it's cold – or it gets cancelled – or my mom doesn't want me to get too wet and cold. We slide everywhere on the field…"

Mrs. Caldas smiles and turns towards the board. She points at the suns that were drawn on that month's calendar. "Ryan, how many days do we have left this week?" Ryan counted the days out. Mrs. Caldas then turned to another student, "And Paige, how many sunny days have we had so far this month?" Paige answered and this movement helped re-engage the twenty other children. "So, class, who knows how many sunny days we would have all together if all (exaggerated with big hand gestures to show all) the days this week were sunny?" Hands were raised across the classroom.

Mrs. Caldas called on one of the students, who answered correctly. Then, in alignment with keeping the children focused, interested, and the material both relevant and fun, she asked, "Class, do you agree with that answer? If you agree with that answer, please put your thumb up. If you disagree with that answer, please put you thumb down." All students engaged and having fun. To keep it relevant, the SuperTeacher continued. "What will you do if it's sunny tomorrow? I will say that again and I want you all to show me what punctuation that sentence ends with. What will you do if it's sunny tomorrow?" All the students used their arms and hands to make shapes. Most made question marks, but a few made periods or exclamation marks.

Connecting the dots of our five pillars of creativity with this SuperTeacher, you'll likely think: "How can I borrow ideas from what she did, perhaps modify them slightly, and bring them into some part of my world?" As a simple example, I thought about the countless meetings that I've had the chance to sit through in my life. Typical engagement of meeting attendees is certainly not close to

100%! A few of Mrs. Caldas' approaches to pulling people into the conversation could have had a powerful effect. What questions do we ask ourselves while we sit in our meetings? How could I make this meeting meaningful for myself and others? How could I keep people reminded of the purpose? How could I diplomatically engage the disengaged?

I was coaching two leaders from two very large organizations recently and had the chance to sit through a meeting that needed one slight change to create a radically improved result. As I observed, I couldn't help but think that this was a textbook meeting. Tasks, action items, and strategies were discussed with accountabilities, due dates, follow-up points all clearly mapped out. The agenda was crystal clear and the group even kept everything very punctual. There was a significant amount of healthy debate around strategies. Voices were heard. Each person left that meeting with clarity of who, what, when, and where. But as the group got up to leave, I had an unsettling feeling. I was there to watch the interaction and watch how the two leaders that I was coaching worked in the meeting setting. The unsettling feeling grew stronger and stronger. Everything – just about everything – went very well. There was tremendous clarity, simplicity, very good communication. The meeting was run like clockwork. What could have been missing? At the conclusion, we all stood up to depart, but a few people remained to converse with each other. I stayed, but just stood there and stared off into space, wondering about this unsettling feeling. Then it hit me. There was only one thing missing, but that one thing was a big thing – maybe the biggest thing. Never once in this meeting did we discuss *why*. Why are we doing this? What's the point? What's the purpose? What's our cause? It didn't need to take 20 minutes, 40 minutes, or even 5 minutes. It could have been a one or two minute story, perhaps even just a 30-second story. As Mrs. Caldas had demonstrated so frequently and effectively, a quick statement or question could bring powerful relevance, purpose, passion, and the *why* back to into everything we had discussed. It could have been a 30-second statement at the beginning, end, or at any point during the meeting. It could have been spoken by one person, any one person. It was a meeting for a very well-known healthcare non-profit and the attendees included leaders from several multi-billion dollar organizations, including a professional sports team. Any attendee could have said something as simple, yet powerful and emotional as: "Thanks to the work of this organization, my grandmother got 3 extra years of life. In those extra three years, she got to know my children and they got to know her. She gave them memories that they will never forget. They still sing the songs she taught them. What we're doing matters." Twenty seconds? Maybe that could be accompanied by a picture, a quick video clip of the children singing one of the songs, a few words printed into the agenda, or a quote from another person whose life was touched by the organization's work. There are dozens of ways to keep the why in front of ourselves, our families, our schools, and our organizations.

One coaching client of mine builds "Mission Moments" into their regular meetings. They may randomly pick an attendee who gets to share a recent example of living the company's mission.

I've reflected on this quite frequently and found that I forget to keep the why in front of myself. There is a famous Latin phrase: *Nemo dat quod non habet.* "You can't give what you don't have." Isn't it worth being creative, collecting ideas around ways you can keep your heart, mind, and soul full of passion and in pursuit of a worthwhile goal? Fill it so you can give it away!

A special thank you to Mrs. Caldas and all the super teachers out there for happening to the world in such a magical way!

Howard's Coffee Idea

When Starbucks hired Howard in 1982, they were doing "pretty good." I use that expression because we hear a version of it from people, families, organizations – and even ourselves – all the time. How's work? Pretty good. How's the family? Pretty good. How was your weekend? Pretty good. How's your football team looking for next season? Pretty good. We may substitute other words in the response, but good, okay, fine, not bad, and alright seem to be the most popular. Jim Collins starts his best-selling book, *Good to Great* with one sentence. "Good is the enemy of great." I recently read an excellent book called *Small Giants* that counters the premise of Collins' book by asking, what if you want to build a sustainably great organization that is intentionally not that big? What if total revenue, net profit, growth, number of customers, and global brand recognition are not part of your definition of a great organization? What if a local non-profit defines greatness as building powerful bonds with those it serves? What if creating a sustainably incredible experience for your customers matters more than increasing the number of customers? What if building a great place to work takes precedence over any other business metric? By any of these definitions, Howard was more interested in the pursuit of greatness than the pursuit of pretty good.

In 1982, Starbucks had just 4 locations. Selling what? Not cups of coffee. They sold all sorts of roasted coffee beans, coffee grinders, coffee makers. Customers brought their purchases home and made their own coffee. Business was going well, and Howard was hired as director of marketing and operations. Part of Howard's job: exploring equipment, roasting styles, and beans – often in other parts of the world.

On his first trip to Italy in 1983, Howard fell in love with the Italian coffee culture. Near his Milan hotel were several coffee houses where locals would gather for an espresso, cappuccino, latte, or macchiato. These coffee houses had an atmosphere that Howard could feel, taste, and smell.

Upon returning to Seattle, he couldn't get the idea out of his head. He was convinced that a version of the Italian coffee culture could be replicated in the United States and he tried to convince the Starbucks founders to do just that. For over a year, Howard pitched his idea repeatedly. When he finally wore them down in 1984, they allowed Howard to set up a small kiosk in the corner of one location to sell prepared coffee drinks. The rest of this shop would operate the way Starbucks had for all twelve years of the company's existence, selling coffee beans and equipment for the customer to make their own coffee at home. Howard understood our 5% rule. He understood that what worked in Italy might need to be modified for the United States. Americans might want a bigger cup of coffee and they just might want it to go. Venti is Italian for twenty, and Americans loved their twenty-ounce cup of coffee to go. Howard's experiment generated more revenue on its first day of business than any Starbucks location in the company's history! Were the founders convinced? Yes! And No!

Howard hoped the success of this small kiosk within a traditional Starbucks store would convince the founders to expand on his idea. He was wrong. They didn't have the same vision for the company and over the next year, Howard drummed up investment capital to the tune of about $1.5 million to start a new company, *Il Giornale*, that would bring the Italian coffee culture to America. He left Starbucks. Howard's *Il Giornale* stores sold coffee drinks made with beans roasted by Starbucks. In fact, the Starbucks founders were among the financial backers supporting the launch of *Il Giornale*. Two years later and after Howard's passion helped him accumulate an additional $4.5 million in venture capital, Howard bought Starbucks from the founders and merged the two companies to form the Starbucks Coffee Company. They put some clothing on the mermaid logo and the rest, as they say, is history.

What did Howard Schultz do differently than most of us? He asked – no *pursued* – different questions. He exposed himself to some ideas from different cultures and allowed himself to wonder how those ideas might fit into the American culture. He modified the ideas as appropriate. He spent more time within the Innovator's Equation than most of us. $\_ + \_ = 10$? He asked, "What would I love to create?" before asking, "What resources are required to create it?" Most initial investors stated clearly that they bought Howard's passion much more than his idea. They weren't so convinced that the general public would be willing to spend $2 on a cup of coffee when the typical cup of coffee in the mid 1980s came from a glass coffee stained so dark it wasn't always easy to see if it was empty or full and sold for about fifty cents. Who would pay 4 times that? They invested in Howard's passion. His passionate pursuit of a question. His quest!

If Howard can do this, maybe you can, too. Decades after Howard Schultz put non-fat latte's in the American vocabulary, I was operating a kid's fitness business and our employees were virtually all under the age of twenty-five. There seemed to be a language barrier. "You're on the schedule for Thursday at 8:00 am" somehow translated into *Make it if you can on Thursday. If you can't, send a text by 8:45 saying* "Didn't make it! ☺." Not on the same page? We didn't have the same dictionary!

I was struggling with a few of these questions:

- Is it even possible to get a motivated staff of part-timers?
- How do we find employees with high standards?
- What can we do to keep them engaged?
- Staff interaction was crucial to success. Is it even possible to create an incredible experience every time?
- How can we get highly engaged staff who really care without full-time management presence?

These questions kept me up at night. With young children as our customers, our prime business hours were all day Saturday and Sunday (birthday parties) and Monday through Friday from 9am until noon. Between noon and 2 or 3pm, our customers were eating lunch and napping. It was possible to hold fitness classes after naptime, but staffing and labor devoured the margins.

Progress came after we started to use all 5 pillars of creativity. We convinced ourselves that it was possible, that someone was already doing something like what we hoped to do, and that we could borrow and modify their ideas, failing forward until it worked. Ultimately, we decided to pursue a different series of questions: Who is great at engaging part-time staff to deliver consistently excellent customer experiences? What could we learn from them and how would we need to modify their strategies? One answer was Starbucks. How did they do it? How could we modify their lessons?

Involvement equals engagement. The opposite is also true. Daniel Pink in his book, *Drive*, says that "Control leads to compliance; autonomy leads to engagement." He teaches that autonomy, or freedom, of four T's will increase engagement.

Time – Task – Technique – Team

Starbucks provides freedom of Task and Technique within a framework. They call it the "Five Ways of Being", which are: *Be Genuine, Welcoming, Involved, Considerate, & Knowledgeable!*

The ways of being are the framework. How these "ways" are accomplished falls under autonomy or freedom of task and technique. Each associate has a great deal of freedom regarding *how* to *Be Welcoming*. As I was studying this and trying to solve this challenge, I also had a consulting client who loved to visit the Starbucks near his office. We would often meet over a cup of coffee.

To make my research real, I started asking the staff in this coffee shop all kinds of questions.

One day, a young lady who was working the drive through excitedly called me over. She just had to show me something. She said, "You know how you're always asking us questions?"

"Yes."

"Well, look at this!" She held out a notebook that she had labeled "Be Welcoming!" and quickly flipped through the pages. Each page had hand-written notes, but she was turning pages too frantically for me to read the content. Then she stopped and blurted out, "Here! That's him! That's your friend, Jim!" Jim was the executive who visited their store almost every day. His name was printed at the top and the entire page was full of notes about Jim. She had written things about what Jim liked to order, the length of his commute, the car he drove, his daughter's interest in sports and college visits, guests who often accompanied Jim on his Starbucks visits – there she laughed loudly and pointed to the middle of the page. "Look! Look! That's you!" Her hand-written notes listed a few of Jim's co-workers and then it said, "Tall guy." The words were crossed out and just above "~~Tall guy~~" she had written "Jonathan." I made it in the notebook.

Wow! I was impressed. Each page had similar notes about regular customers. She knew them. She cared enough to take notes. She would often flip through the book to review people that she knew. They were no longer just customers to her. They were people. Individual people. Often, this young barista would recognize a car as it pulled up to the drive through and modify her greeting to the driver accordingly. "Hey Jim! How did your daughter like UConn?" She knew that Jim's daughter was considering the University of Connecticut and had visited the college over the weekend.

She was beaming as she explained that her manager had recently asked her to show her notebook to the whole team at that location. The team had dedicated the entire week to a focus on "Be

Welcoming" and this barista was one of several asked to share her approach to this way of being. She spoke to her peers about her strategy and read excerpts from her notebook. What the manager did not do next is gold. The manager did NOT say, "I've purchased notebooks for everyone. We're all going to do this now." She did NOT say, "Take notes on your regular customers from here on." That Starbucks store manager simply said, "Wow! That is an awesome example of *Be Welcoming!*" Some members of the team decided to take better notes about their regular customers. Some decided to simply ask more questions of customers to get to know them better. Some decided to pick one customer each day or week to get to know a little better. Some decided to share free scone samples near the store entrance a few times each day. Autonomy. Freedom. Within a framework of 5 ways of being. Does it work? Howard Schultz said, "...people think we are a great marketing company, but in fact we spend very little money on marketing and more money on training our people than advertising."

Back to the children's fitness business. I shared a brief summary of the 5 ways of being with our employees and asked the group, "What are our *ways of being*?" We discussed it regularly over the course of several weeks to think about it. The team arrived at three ways of being: *Be Enthusiastic, Be Encouraging, Be Loving* and eventually added a fourth: *Be 100% Responsible for an Amazing Experience!*

5%. The Ways of Being needed some modification for that business. I expect it will for you, as well. Where will you apply it? At work? With a project team? In your classroom? In your family? For a sports team you coach or a scout troop you lead? Perhaps you simply get started with just one way of being. You might pick a second next week, month, or year. Freedom within a framework. Involvement. Engagement. Iteration. I've worked with leaders who build one way of being into one day a month. Simple. When do you start?

The Boy Who Chased Cars

The very first time Soichiro saw a car drive through his small village, he ran after it. What else would a curious young boy do? What would he do if he caught it? Soichiro ran until he reached a spot in the road where the car had leaked a very small amount of fluid, perhaps oil or gas. He put his finger in the substance and smelled it. Soichiro was delighted! And he was hooked! He wanted to know more about this vehicle, how it worked, what it could do, everything. A few years later he sought a job as an apprentice in a mechanic shop, convincing the owner of the shop that, despite his young age, he would be the best worker there. And he was. Before long, his curiosity, which he fed regularly, led him to look for more problems to solve. In his twenties, he started his own small automotive repair shop, that smell of oil still in his blood. The small business wasn't very successful until he developed a new wheel for the car, one with metal spokes instead of wood. After this, sales of metal spoke automotive wheels around the world created a significant stream of income for the young man's business. Then, at the age of thirty, Soichiro decided that he would manufacture piston rings. His first big customer was a company we all know: Toyota. Unfortunately, of first fifty piston rings delivered to Toyota, forty-seven were rejected for quality issues. To Soichiro, failure was just feedback, so he decided to enroll at a technical institute nearby. After 2 years, he was expelled for not taking any exams. Failure? Not to Soichiro. He wouldn't get a diploma, but continued attending classes for a 3rd year and described it through the lens of a world-class innovator:

"[A diploma is] worth less than a movie ticket. With the ticket, you can at least enter the movie house and spend an enjoyable evening; but a diploma is by no means a sure ticket

to life. I don't give a damn for the diploma. What I want is the knowledge. "

While taking courses at the Institute, he also visited dozens of nearby factories to imitate Isaac Newton in "standing on the shoulders of giants." He was an idea sponge, seeking out and absorbing lessons and strategies from everywhere. He wasn't interested in the symbol of learning, only the actual learning, the knowledge. Therein lies a great series of questions for all of us to ask ourselves:

- Where can I most effectively acquire the knowledge, wisdom, and experience that I need?
- In what ways do I let the world's assumptions limit me?
- If __ + __ = 10, what are some options for obtaining the ingredients I'm currently missing?

Soichiro described some of the ups and downs of his journey this way: "I would have to put in the necessary time, but nothing could stop me from succeeding. I just wouldn't give in, no way... There are qualities that lead to success. Courage, perseverance – profound belief in something allows every individual to find an immense inner force and to uncover his or her failings. I let no one disturb my concentration... Even hunger could not disturb me."

Over the next few years, his company rapidly gained the reputation for being the best manufacturer of piston rings in the area and, shortly after World War II ended, he sold the piston ring manufacturing company to Toyota. When they closed the deal, Soichiro told one of the Toyota managers that he planned to take a *human holiday*. That is exactly what he did. This *human holiday* lasted for about a year and he enjoyed life throughout those months perhaps a bit more indulgently than most of us ever do.

One afternoon, Soichiro's wife, Sachi, returned from a long bike ride exhausted and frustrated. She had been bicycling around the neighboring villages in search of rice on the black market. In post-World War II Japan, rice, along with many other items, wasn't always easy to acquire. When she returned, she approached Soichiro and vented a bit of frustration, saying, "For once, you try going out and buying the rice." He didn't like that idea, but, instead promised to attach a motor to her bicycle. Rice wasn't the only thing that was difficult to find in their region of Japan in 1946. Motorcycles and gasoline were also extremely scarce. Soichiro threw himself into the challenge and, over the next several months he affixed a motorized drive to Sachi's bicycle. He found an abundant supply of free engines – one of the radios used during the war came with its own gas engine for a generator. These radios were abandoned and littered throughout most Japanese towns. In place of gasoline, Soichiro modified the little engine to run on pine resin and found another left over war item – a metal canister for holding water – perfect for a fuel tank.

After delivering his first motorized bicycle to his wife, Sachi, Soichiro went on to make hundreds of similar engine kits that he sold to neighbors and bike shops throughout the region. So ended the human holiday and Soichiro's enthusiasm for making motorized vehicles was accelerated! By the time the supply of free engines was exhausted, Soichiro had decided that he was ready to make the entire motorcycle. He initially set up a little factory making engines that were sold as a kit to be attached to a bicycle, but, within a few years, he was making and selling hundreds and then thousands of motorcycles each year. You may have seen one of his motorcycles on the road. They go by Soichiro Honda's last name. Honda is the largest producer of motorcycles and engines in the world today.

But the path was not a happily ever after fairytale by any means. In 1948, an economic slowdown hurt sales and Soichiro Honda knew he needed to do something. The financial side of the business was occupying too much of his time, energy, and focus. Honda was not willing to let the company go under, saying, "… all those people [employees] who were depending on me... I solemnly said to myself: If I give up now, everyone will die of hunger." He decided it was time to take on a partner. Fujisawa Takeo joined Honda Motor Company as Soichiro's partner. The partnership between Takeo and Honda would turn out to be a classic example of two people each complimenting and adding to the gifts of the other. The question is simple to ask, but demands a profound discipline to consistently pursue: "What are we really trying to accomplish here and what knowledge, resources, people, and strategies will we need to create it?" Where do we need help and what help do we need?

The partnership helped take the company to another level and in 1954, Soichiro decided that he would enter a Honda in the world-famous motorcycle race on the Isle of Man. In the 1950s, Japanese manufacturing had a worldwide reputation of being inferior. Soichiro pursued the question: "What could change that paradigm in one fell swoop?" Winning a world-renowned race was one answer. With all the preparation, Honda's first appearance in the race was 1959. They finished sixth and went back to work. Two years later, Honda motorcycles took the top five positions in both 125cc and 250cc race classes, stunning the world and altering the global perception of Japanese manufacturing. After the victories, one British paper called Honda's engines "the best in the world."

Takeo brought more than just financial management to the company. Inspired by an idea in a book, Takeo proposed that Honda's R&D team have a degree of separation from the distractions of daily business. The book and source of this collected idea, *I Am a Cat*, takes place in a war-torn region. Amid massive distractions, a scientist in the story practically locks himself in his laboratory to study the electrical workings of frog eyeballs. Takeo later wrote, "engineers would benefit from the scientist's isolation – a place so serene that they can conduct their research even when society is in an uproar around them. That way, the engineers can focus on their work without worrying about anything else."

This R&D team almost immediately became interested in making an automobile, so Honda did. In the 1970s, a US amendment to the Clean Air Act would test auto makers ability to follow the innovator's equation. Most responded by fighting the bill, but a dramatic reduction in automobile emissions became law in 1970. Soichiro Honda recalled the Isle of Man motorcycle race and told his staff, "Now is the chance for Honda to take over the world marketplace. Every manufacturer is facing the exact same problem. You can't buy the technology. This is a rare chance... for Honda to pit our ideas and technology against a score of world-class contenders. When it comes to developing new technologies, we can't lose." The team went to work, but one of the most significant problems came from a surprising source – Soichiro Honda, himself.

Soichiro believed the solution would be found via an air-cooled engine, but his engineering team was convinced that it would require a liquid-cooled engine. They went back and forth for some time. Honda, both the man and company, have a long-standing tradition of welcoming debate. Soichiro wouldn't budge. Takeo Fujisawa would once again add immeasurable value to the company.

Fujisawa paid his partner, Soichiro, a visit, telling him, "I'm no engineer so I've stayed out of your way. But there is one question I'd like you to ask yourself. Which path are you planning to take, Honda-san? Are you the president or an engineer? I believe the time has come to clarify your position and I'd like to know what you think." After an extended silence, Soichiro let his partner know that he would chose the role of president, and Fujisawa continued, "It's all right then if the staff works on a water-cooled engine?" Soichiro agreed. Fujisawa added a statement that we can all modify and use. "Honda-san, I want you to know that I'll quit when you quit." This statement assured Soichiro that his partner was in this for the same reasons and didn't have a hidden agenda. Fujisawa had no interest in taking the place of Soichiro. The two partners did eventually retire on the same day.

In 1973, the water-cooled Honda Civic was the first production car to meet the new EPA emission standards. Many in the auto industry continued to fight against the challenge legally, and Soichiro said in an interview, "When Congress passes new emission standards, we hire 50 more engineers and [other car companies] hire 50 more lawyers." To prove that the technology would work on other vehicles – even large engines so popular in the U.S. at the time, Soichiro bought a 1973 V-8 model from one of the Big 3. He shipped it to Japan, designed a new head for the engine using Honda's newly developed solution, and shipped it back to the EPA. The Big 3 V-8 modified by Honda passed the latest emissions requirements.

These words from Soichiro Honda are the best way to end this chapter:

"Success can be achieved only through repeated failure and introspection. In fact, success represents 1 percent of your work which results only from the 99 percent that is called failure."

What About Me?

Two brothers, Richard and Maurice, left New Hampshire and headed out to the west coast, intent on getting involved in the film production business. Why not? It was the beginning of the Great Depression and their dreams of becoming famous producers fizzled in the sunny state. They tried their hands at a small movie theater in the Los Angeles suburbs, but never created a sustainable revenue stream. They had a clear and simple goal: become millionaires by the age of 50. It was not working out. In 1937 they decided to open a hot dog stand in Pasadena, but closed it in 1940. Then, on May 15th, 1940, they opened a bigger restaurant in San Bernadino. This restaurant, with its signature 35 cent meal including a barbecue beef, ham, or pork sandwich and fries, would be their meal ticket. Before long, sales surpassed $200,000 per year, or about $4.2 million in 2023 dollars. The brothers were on their way. The vast menu included chili, tamales, grilled cheese, ham, baked beans, root beer floats, giant malts, and even peanut butter and jelly sandwiches. Although the BBQ joint did have a few stools, carhops served most of the food to customers who didn't have to leave their cars. On the top of the menu were the cursive words, "We Barbecue All Meats in Our Own Barbecue Pit".

But Richard and Maurice decided to ask a different question in 1948. They asked questions like: what's really driving this? How could we simplify? What would be scalable? Then, they shut the doors. They closed their money-making machine for three months. When they reopened, the new menu was simplified. It contained just 9 items. Hamburger, cheeseburger, fries, and six drink options: milk shake, coca cola, root beer, orange drink, milk, and coffee. Their process for making and serving these nine items was a choreographed dance. The brothers had mapped out the revamped restaurant kitchen on their back yard tennis court and worked through every layout and cooking operation to create an efficient process. Why? What would lead the brothers to mess with a good thing? They took a good look at the numbers and discovered that 80% of their BBQ restaurant business was hamburgers. Their willingness to question success the way they did led to sales surpassing $350,000 by the early 1950s.

In 1954, they would cross paths with Ray, another creative businessman with an interesting background. Ray was from Illinois, had lied about his age so that he could serve in WW2 after going through boot camp with none other than Walt Disney (who had also lied about his age to enroll in the war effort a year before he was eligible), and was a man of many professions. Rays resume included: paper cup salesman, pianist, DJ, realtor, and milkshake machine salesman. Ray met the brothers because their busy restaurant used 8 of his Multimixer milkshake machines. Each Multimixer could make six milkshakes at a time, meaning the brothers' small octagonal walk-up restaurant could make 48 milk shakes simultaneously. 48 milk shakes at the same time in one restaurant! That number got Ray's attention, so he paid the brothers a visit. He parked his car in the lot shortly before the lunch rush and watched in awe as the restaurant's precise choreography handled an impressively large number of regular walk-up customers. Ray's excitement grew and over dinner that night, Ray suggested that the brothers expand their operation and open additional locations. They had already tried this on a very small scale, licensing their concept to a few franchisees, but with marginal success. Ray recalls their conversation about the massive potential that he saw:

"I've been in the kitchens of a lot of restaurants and drive-ins selling Multimixers around the country," I told them, "and I have never seen anything to equal the potential of this place of yours. Why don't you open a series of units like this? It would be a gold mine for you and for me, too, because

every one would boost my Multimixer sales. What d'you say?"

Silence.

I felt like I'd dragged my tie in my soup or something. The two brothers just sat there looking at me. Then Mac gave that little wince that sometimes passes for a smile in New England and turned around in his chair to point up at the hill overlooking the restaurant.

"See that big white house with the wide front porch?" he asked. "That's our home and we love it. We sit out on the porch in the evenings and watch the sunset and look down on our place here. It's peaceful. We don't need any more problems. We are in a position to enjoy life now, and that's just what we intend to do."

His approach was utterly foreign to my thinking, so it took me a few minutes to reorganize my arguments. But it soon became apparent that further discussion along that line would be futile, so I said they could have their cake and eat it too by getting somebody else to open the other places for them. I could still peddle my Multimixers in the chain.

"It'll be a lot of trouble," Dick objected. "Who could we get to open them for us?"

I sat there feeling a sense of certitude begin to envelope me. Then I leaned forward and said, "Well, what about me?"

What about me, indeed! Ray and the brothers did decide to work together. But you've already guessed that. In New York City on November 30, 1984, Richard McDonald was ceremoniously served the 50,000,000,000th (yes, 50 *Billionth*) burger served by a company known around the world simply by the last name of the two brothers, Richard and Maurice: McDonald's. What about me!!!

What about you?

Three Months to do What?

From April to June of 1955, Ray Kroc would live, breathe, and sleep one simple mission. How do we perfect the french fry? Kroc had opened his first McDonald's near Chicago and the fries just were not the same. Why not? His experiments would take into account just about everything: potato type, oil type, oil temperature, salt, cooling process, pre-blanching of the potatoes, storage environment. The storage environment played a big role. In San Bernadino, the potatoes were stored outside and the dry desert air changed the potatoes. How do you replicate that near Chicago? Answer: You experiment intensely for three months! When I think about that, I am a bit uncomfortable. Why? I look at aspects of my life, my leadership, my parenting, and ask: "Have I invested three intensely focused months on learning and experimenting to master this area?" This applies to some of the simplest concepts of our lives, like listening, facilitating great conversations, getting the kids out the door for school, having simple – yet delicious and healthy – dinner options, and so many more areas. Three months... What if you picked just one aspect of your life and gave it that level of attention?

Ray Kroc didn't stop at the perfect fry. He pursued many great questions, including:

- What if we own the land under the restaurants? (In a speech to a business school, Kroc asked: "What business am I in?" Hamburgers? No. Franchising? No. "Real estate!" One attendee heard that and iterated, starting a car wash chain where he owned the real estate under the car wash locations.)

- How can we harness the best ideas of each franchisee?

- How can we build a business where no one can fail, where anyone willing to work hard and follow our process will succeed, no matter where they are located?

- How can I set up a business relationship where my partners are in business for themselves, but not by themselves? ...where anyone can succeed? ...where the taste is consistent from Alaska to Alabama?
- What kind of mantra, motto, or slogan would help keep us on track?
- How do we ensure that the franchisees know we have their best interests at heart?

Kroc frequently repeated the mantra: "Either we're green and growing or ripe and rotting." You're green and growing as a parent, leader, entrepreneur, friend, spouse... or ripe and rotting!

"If I had a brick for every time I've repeated the phrase Quality, Service, Cleanliness and Value, I think I'd probably be able to bridge the Atlantic Ocean with them." – Ray Kroc.

McDonald's and Your Journey

Most businesses ask how they can simplify their business, or what the true goals are, but the McDonald's brothers pursued these questions. Most of us occasionally ask ourselves what we should consider saying *No!* to, but the McDonald's brothers pursued this in 1948 and again during that conversation with Ray Kroc in 1954. Their goals and his goals weren't aligned. The McDonald brothers seem to have asked themselves, "What are we looking for?" Their pursuit of simplicity and a decrease in stress reminds me of a line from one of my favorite authors, Peter Kreeft. Kreeft has written about 100 books and was asked which one was his favorite. His wise answer: "The one I didn't write when my children were young." What matters most and what matters least are excellent questions to revisit regularly. Andrew Carnegie, for example, dedicated the first half of his life to amassing a fortune and the second half to giving it away. One of Carnegie's contributions: the building of 2,509 libraries between 1883 and 1929. Carnegie said,

"I choose free libraries as the best agencies for improving the masses of the people, because they give nothing for nothing. They only help those who help themselves."

I often meet people who tell me about something that needs to change. They often say something like, "I wish that were different..." I'm reminded of Ray's dinner conversation with the McDonald brothers... "What about me?" What if you found something that needs changing and you initiated the change? Perhaps a good path to consider is finding someone who's already begun a mission that is aligned with yours, ask where they need help, and offer, "What about me?"

Little D's New Habit Strategy

His name wasn't really *Little D*, but that's what I chose to call him. I get to spend time with the youth leaders of an incredible organization, Alvin Ailey Dance Foundation's AileyCamp. I always like to share real lessons from real people and was sure that the person I called *Little D* would be both memorable and helpful for their journeys. Over and over I am reminded that a memorable story can stick with people and help them make changes, often years after they first hear the story.

But... if the story is to make an impact, the story has to stick. So I tried to add some stickiness to Little D's story. The AileyCamp youth leaders came primarily from what many would consider underprivileged backgrounds. Most did not have significant family income, and some were even homeless. As described on their website, "AileyCamp targets students with academic, social and domestic challenges—criteria that often determine a child's risk of dropping out of school—but also welcomes students who have little opportunity to develop their artistic interests." I try hard not to make automatic assumptions about what an advantage or disadvantage might be. My reasoning: some perceived disadvantages can be advantages and vice versa. In my own life, failures and a lack of perceived resources have most often been the best motivators, caused me to seek a very creative solution. A naturally talented athlete may never learn to work hard. A person with a great job may never start that business they've always dreamed of. A study of self-made millionaires in the U.K. found that 40 percent were dyslexic. Richard Branson is in that 40 percent. Malcolm Gladwell's thought-provoking book, *David and Goliath*, challenges our thinking: "There is a set of advantages that have to do with material resources, and there is a set that have to do with the absence of material resources – and the reason underdogs win as often as they do is that the latter is sometimes every bit the equal of the former."

Was Little D an underdog? When he was just seven years old, Little D's parents passed away, leaving him to be raised by three legal guardians. Little D's father had built a successful business and the inheritance was quite substantial. By the time Little D celebrated his 18th birthday, the guardians claimed that there was no money left from the inheritance.

An Uncommon Training Program

Little D decided to take the guardians to court; however, the laws of his village required that he represent himself. This meant he would have to build his case, communicate his case, and handle questions from the judge and guardians. All of this would be done in public with an audience. Little D was incredibly uncomfortable with this idea. Throughout his eighteen years of life, he stuttered. He was not comfortable speaking to groups. His voice was very soft. He tended to ramble. He would become short of breath very easily when speaking. Little D had a decision to make. Give up or do something. AileyCamp teaches several daily affirmations. I love this one: "I will not use the word can't to define my possibilities." Little D would agree with this mantra.

He found a book of famous speeches. He read it. Then he read it again. And again. And again. He not only read the book many times, but he copied the entire book by hand eight times and memorized segments of it that he would recite over and over again. He was learning how to use words to persuade. But Little D's problem was much deeper than just having words to use. He stuttered. His voice was weak. His lungs were weak. "*I will not use the word can't to define my possibilities.*" Little D walked along the seashore, reciting segments from the book aloud, over the sound of the waves. He put pebbles in his mouth as he pronounced the words loudly over the sound of crashing waves. His enunciation improved and he began to build up his lungs. Progress.

But Little D's obstacles were not entirely overcome. Little D also had a habit of laziness, and often found himself skipping his speech training. Despite committing himself and re-committing himself, the laziness habit was winning. You could say that Little D just couldn't get himself to do the work, but you would be wrong. Little D *refused to let can't define his possibilities*. He revisited his commitment of preparation to speak in court and decided to live in a small cave on the side of a cliff by the ocean. This might help eliminate the distractions of going into town to hang out. So now, Little D was living in a small cave with no running water. He knew that he needed to enhance his training. How could he more effectively build up his lungs, voice, stamina, and enunciation? He started jogging along the ocean, reciting segments of the book aloud with pebbles in his mouth. The training was working. Next, he incorporated running up and down the hills by the beach – still speaking with pebbles in his mouth.

Laziness was not so easily overcome. Although he was living in a cave and couldn't really bathe properly, Little D still found himself wandering into town on occasion and he knew that his time for preparation was running short. Little D found a unique method for maintaining focus and motivation. He shaved sections of his head in such a way that he no longer wanted to be seen in public until it grew back. Laziness and distractions overpowered!

After all his training and creative problem-solving, Little D had his day in court. He spoke clearly and brilliantly and he won! The judge ordered the guardians to give Little D about $7 million from his father's estate. Unfortunately, the guardians no longer had any money. Even though Little D won the case, he received no money. Was all his effort for naught? Little D not only won the case, but people who heard him speak that day were so impressed that many hired him to teach them to speak and to write or give speeches for them. Little D would go on to become one of the most famous orators of his time. No longer Little D, Demosthenes of Athens would also become one of the most effective speakers against the tyranny of Philip of Macedon and Alexander the Great.

How's your training program going? What gets in your way? What will you do with Little D's story? Will you share it? Will you let can't define your possibilities?

Yes, Popcorn Kernels!

The young Boy Scout was so excited that he ran around the table and pulled his friend over to show him what they had just sold. A bag of popcorn kernels! 30 ounces. Almost two pounds – of popcorn *kernels*. These were not popped, not chocolate or caramel covered, nor were they even quick pop or microwaveable. The boys had sold a bag full of nothing but unpopped kernels. This had never been done before and their excitement was contagious.

"Whoooaaah!!" was the jaw-dropping awe-inspired response of the second boy. Both boys knew this was a big deal. From the looks on their faces and the way they discussed this sale, I could tell that they would be repeating the heroics of this sale many times that day and for days to come. But why? Why was selling a bag of popcorn such a big deal to these boys?

The two Boy Scouts were so caught up in the celebration that they almost missed their next few potential customers. Their table was set up in the entranceway to a grocery store on a busy Friday afternoon and the foot traffic was considerable. Every person that entered or exited the grocery store had to see their table covered with assorted popcorn treats and make eye contact with at least one of the boys. If a passerby paused for long enough, one of the boys would go into the pitch. It wasn't the best pitch I'd ever heard, but it was short, sweet, and fairly effective. Both boys had it down and many shoppers were returning home with some form of popcorn. As I approached the boys, I thought to myself, *If they take some initiative to make a sale, I'll buy something. If they just sit there and don't say anything, I'm not going to reward that. It's great for kids to take initiative in learning how to market and sell something of value.* After looking through their product offerings and listening to the boy's short explanation of each, I knew exactly which one I wanted. When I first told the boy I would take a bag of plain kernels, his response was one of questioning disbelief. His eyes almost betrayed his thought: "Are... you... sure?"

I bought the bag and thought about ways to make this a more meaningful interaction. Many years ago, right after I finished college, I had the chance to go through one of the world's most famous leadership development programs (designed by a company with the initials GE). A mentor in the program talked about creating a habit of collecting TPOVs (Teachable Points of View) or LPOVs (Leadership Points of View). We were encouraged to seek, find, create, and share teachable moments. They could be in the form of a story, metaphor, model, or even a bag of popcorn. Look for lessons and share them. This TPOV habit sharpens two of the most important leadership traits: hunger and humility. We looked for lessons we needed, tried to apply them, and built a formidable collection of tools to use in teaching others. I've tried to maintain the habit and hone it for many years, at times much more consciously than others. After my popcorn purchase, I kept thinking through the TPOV angle. What were some lessons from this and how could I best share them? I quickly thought about some easy ways to make this into a lesson for the Boy Scouts. I asked them why they thought I purchased this bag and why no one else had. My follow up questions related to what value I might see in the bag of un-popped kernels and how they might be able to communicate this value best to other buyers. I asked if they might want to set up a sales experiment to test what we had just learned together. They seemed intrigued by the discussion.

A few days later I had the chance to share some of the popcorn lessons (TPOV) with an incredible group of high school students who are members of the Future Business Leaders of America (FBLA). A very effective use of TPOV is to teach the lesson several times right after you've experienced the lesson. This not only cements the lesson into your own life, but also reveals additional lessons, helps you find the better ways to teach it, and gives people in your life the opportunity to learn something from your experience. A mentor of mine used to say, "If you haven't read a book or learned a new lesson in the last two weeks, you likely don't have much of interest to share with those around you." Great teachers are great learners. Don't arrive!

With the group of several hundred FBLA members, I shared the popcorn story and then invited them to help use some of the five creative pillars. We explored some questions:

- Why had no one else bought this popcorn?
- Should pricing be evaluated?
- What words, phrases, tone, stories, images might help sell the un-popped kernels?
- What was the driving motivation for the kernel buyer?
- Could this motivation be translated in a meaningful way to captivate other potential kernel buyers?
- What locations might completely change the game?
- What about times of day or promotions?
- What might 2x, 10x, or 20x sales per hour?
- Who could we get involved that would dramatically affect our sales?
- Would a game, prize, auction, or raffle help?
- What endorsements or links to celebrity/events/history could we consider?
- If the boys needed to sell ten of these kernel bags within an hour (or ten minutes), how could they do it?

Following Einstein's advice, we spent considerable time working on the best questions to ask for attacking this problem. I then asked the FBLA members to create options. Many options. We selected one question: "How could we sell that same 30 oz bag of popcorn for $20, $50, or even $100 or more?" then created options, some bad, some good, some very bad, and some very good. The goal was simply to create a quantity of options, and we frequently added or changed the question in order to keep the process going. I like to think about this process as "Build-build-build-build-build-jump!" It simply means take one idea and explore several very similar ideas, then jump to a very different idea and repeat. A few simple and very effective question to keep this type of exercise going: "What is a similar idea?" For example, one of the ideas was to change the state of the product. Pop the kernels and sell them in small bags. What are some similar ideas? Pop the kernels and sell them one at a time, or sell one for a coin of any type. Pop the kernels and have a few dipping mixtures, one could be chocolate, one honey, and one a holiday spice with nutmeg and cinnamon. Pop the kernels and set up a roulette wheel with bag size on the wheel. Charge one dollar for each spin with a chance of getting a very small bag, a medium bag, a very large bag, or no bag. This option could certainly lead to many other similar options. Charge different amounts for a number of spins. Pop the corn and sell a limitless bag of popcorn while the customer is shopping. They need only bring their bag back to the front for a fill-up. Partner with the grocery store to add a drink option. Put the individual kernels in a paper bag with only one colored green. Charge $1 per kernel a shopper wants to blindly select. If they get the green kernel, the Boy Scouts will do their shopping for them or carry all their groceries, or mow their lawn, or... Perhaps this change to a game or raffle is followed by many iterations built on games and raffles. Customers could buy a small bag for $1 or pay $5 for the same bag with a chance to win a second popcorn item for free. After building many options around this theme, the next jump might be to athletics, famous people, or art. Build-build-build-build-jump! Use questions to keep it similar and then to change the theme or topic completely. Use questions to create limits and then to remove limits. What if we could get a famous athlete to endorse or sign one bag (or each bag)? What if we could get local musicians or athletes to sign the bags? Give it a try. Remember, practicing creativity is a lot like exercising a muscle or cardio workouts. The more you practice, the easier it gets and the stronger you become. As John Steinbeck put it, "'Ideas are like rabbits. You get a couple and learn how to handle them, and pretty soon you have a dozen."

What was my motivation for buying the bag of kernels? Initially, it was simple. I saw the bag of popcorn kernels as a great teaching tool to help my daughters better understand emotional intelligence (EI). To share our TPOV, my daughters invited friends to do the experiment and even built a video of the experience. It's just one of many exercises we've done around EI and certainly not just for kids! After the interchange with the Boy Scouts and FBLA, I added several additional options to my list of lessons. Maybe Steinbeck was right: Ideas are like rabbits!

Amelia & the ROI of Inspiration

She vanished without a trace. She was one of the most famous people in the world and then, on July 2nd, 1937, just a few weeks shy of her 40th birthday, she simply disappeared. Millions of dollars were spent searching for her. Theories abound. Did she crash into the ocean, survive on a small Pacific island, become the first American POW captured by the Japanese leading up to WWII, or disappear from the public eye, change her identity and live a secret, but relatively normal life in New Jersey? She was described in her high school yearbook as "the girl who walked alone" and walk alone she did, only with millions of people watching.

Her story, like each or ours, is full of both lessons and warnings. When Amelia Earhart was just seven-years-old, her father, Edwin, took her to the 1903 World's Fair in St. Louis. The trip would be expensive, as it required 300 miles of train, meals, and lodging. Amelia's maternal grandfather was a wealthy judge and considered the trip to be an appalling waste of money for the financially strapped young family. Despite his father-in-law's perspective, Edwin eventually convinced the judge to lend them money for the trip. Amelia came home from that World's Fair with her imagination set on fire! What is the ROI of inspiration? After the fair, Amelia and her uncle built a small wooden roller coaster from the shed roof in her backyard. Yes, it did crash, on the very first run!

Food for thought… when you're hungry, what do you do? When you're thirsty, what do you do? Eat. Drink. Right? When you're not inspired, what do you do? Just about nothing! Sit on the couch. Watch TV. Surf the web. And that leads to inspiration? Not so often. Edwin Earhart understood that a trip to the World's Fair could be a priceless experience. Instead of doing nothing, he helped expand the vision and inspiration of his family! As Ralph Waldo Emerson wisely quipped: "The mind, once stretched by a new idea, never returns to its original dimensions."

As a child, Amelia sledded in the snow via belly-flopping – considered the tomboy way and unbecoming of girls at the time. She studied bugs, caught snakes, collected pictures and magazine articles of women she respected and admired (including explorers, physicians, psychologists, fire lookouts, and theater directors). She loved to read. Amelia's father, Edwin, had a job that required a lot of travel, so the family moved around a lot. Amelia attended six different high schools. Later in life, when people would say "I'm from your hometown," Amelia would ask, "Which one?" Some might consider moving around as detrimental, but she appreciated the experience. The mind, once stretched by a new idea...! Traveling as a child inspired Amelia to want to see more of the world. She would even play a make-believe game called "Boogie" with her little sister, Muriel. They would climb up into a carriage and imagine they were riding on elephants or camels and exploring faraway places like Africa. For her 11th birthday, her dad took her to the Iowa State Fair where she saw her first airplane.

Amelia, however, didn't fall in love with flying until the winter of 1918. While working in Toronto as a Red Cross Nurse's Aid, she conversed with dozens of injured military pilots about their flying experiences. That same winter, Earhart later recalled: *"For the first time I realized what the World War meant. Instead of new uniforms and brass bands, I saw only the results of four years' desperate struggle; men without arms and legs, men who were paralyzed, and men who were blind. One day I saw four one-legged men at once, walking as best they could down the street together."* This powerful experience contributed to Earhart becoming a lifelong pacifist who frequently spoke on the topic.

While in Toronto, Amelia spent considerable time watching the Royal Flying Corps practicing at a nearby airfield. When one pilot flew low over the stands, most onlookers ducked for cover, but Amelia stood her ground, fixated on the flying machine and saying, "His little red airplane said something to me as it swished by." She was hooked. Amelia noted in her biography, "I remember well that when the snow blown back by the propellers stung my face I felt the first urge to fly. I tried to get permission to go up, but the rules forbade.... the memory of the planes remains clearly, and the sense of the inevitability of flying... Those months in Toronto aroused my interest in flying." The mind, once stretched by a new idea...! Amelia was a passenger for her first ten-minute flight in 1920 and, just a few months later, purchased her first plane, "The Canary", on her 24th birthday in 1921. Feeding her sense of adventure, she went on to set all manner of records: speed, altitude, distance. In 1922, she was the first woman to fly solo above 14,000 feet, breaking the altitude record. In 1928, she was the first woman to fly across the Atlantic and sent this telegram to her mother before the flight: "Don't worry. No matter what happens it will have been worth the trying." Since she didn't pilot the plane, Earhart referred to herself as "a sack of potatoes" and said, "maybe someday I'll try it alone.... there's more to life than being a passenger." Fourteen people had already died trying to cross Atlantic, but Amelia was determined to accomplish the flight solo, and did so in 1932, on the exact 5-year anniversary of Lindbergh's 1st trans-Atlantic flight. Unlike her first trans-Atlantic flight, the 1932 plane did not have water pontoons. She had no intentions of landing in water. A storm over the last few hours of that record solo flight debilitated the plane's altimeter and threatened the daring aviator's life. Over the last several hours of the flight, Earhart alternately ascended and descended to keep the wings de-iced and the plane out of the ocean. Heavy clouds and fog meant the ocean wasn't visible until her plane was almost in the water. At one point, when she saw flames coming from the engine manifold and fuel leaking into the cockpit, she decided to set the plane down as soon as land was sighted. The planned destination was Paris, but she shortened the trip a bit and landed instead in a farmer's field in Northern Ireland. A farmhand approached her plane and said, "You're in Gallagher's Pasture. Have you come far?" After nearly 15 hours of flying, Amelia laughed and replied, "I've come from America!"

Amelia didn't stop there. Other accomplishments include speed records, altitude records and many firsts, most notably: first woman solo nonstop coast to coast flight across the U.S., first person to solo 2,408 miles from Hawaii to California, and first woman to attempt to fly around the world.

During her round-the-world flight attempt, shortly before she disappeared, Amelia wrote to her husband, "Please know I'm quite aware of the hazards. I want to do it because I want to do it. Women must try to do things as men have tried. When they fail, failure must be but a challenge to others." Earhart had completed 75% of the circumnavigation and had about 7,000 miles to go.

The most difficult landing target of the entire trip, by far, was Howland Island. Howland is a tiny island in the middle of the South Pacific, only about a half mile wide, 1.5 miles long, and the highest point is only about 10 feet above the sea. On a clear day, the small island might only be visible once Earhart's plane was within about 20 or 30 miles. In order to dramatically increase the chance of making it safely to Howland Island, the original plan had been to fly west. Following the original flight plan, Earhart flew west, from Oakland to Hawaii, and was taking off for Howland Island on March 20, 1937. With her flair for publicity leveraging significant dates, it looked like she might be trying to complete the trip on the exact 10 year anniversary of Lindbergh's first trans-Atlantic flight and 5 year anniversary of her own. During the takeoff attempt departing Hawaii, a mechanical failure caused serious damage to the plane and required that the plane be shipped back to the mainland for significant repairs, which took almost two months. By this point, a decision had to be made. Changes in wind patterns around the globe made traveling east more practical than west. The original plan of travelling west had several significant advantages. If they struggled to spot Howland Island, they would have only flown about 1900 miles and would have plenty of fuel remaining to fly for about 1000 additional miles. This range could be used to search for the island or to continue flying west, where the South Pacific is full of numerous islands that could have served as a backup landing strip. On the other hand, when traveling east, the plane would not arrive at Howland until almost 2600 miles into the trip, allowing much less room for error. In addition, to the east of Howland, there are very few backup landing strips, so overshooting the target when traveling east was much more perilous. Flying west over that same 2600 miles between Howland and New Guinea would provide a massive landing target with plenty of large islands as backup landing strips leading up to the coast of New Guinea.

On July 2nd, Amelia disappeared after these radio transmissions:

0646: "Take a bearing. About 200 miles out. Position doubtful."
0742: "We must be on you but cannot see you, gas running low. Unable to reach you by radio. Flying at 1000 feet."

Over the next 17 days, the greatest organized effort ever undertaken in behalf of a lost flier included 9 ships, over 60 aircraft, 160 sailors, searched an estimated 262,281 square miles of ocean (roughly the size of the state of Texas), and cost $4 million (about $80 million in 2023 currency). Most search efforts were spent looking for wreckage floating in the water. Nearby Islands were searched, but primarily by flying over and looking for debris of an aircraft. No ground searches were conducted on any nearby islands.

Some details from that infamous last trip:

32 flights, average flight: 893 miles
20 flights were under 1,000 miles
Only 2 flights over 2,000 miles (5 flights over 1,400 miles)
The 4 longest flights:
     2556 miles (Lae, New Guinea to Howland Island)
     2410 miles (Hawaii to Oakland, California)

1961 miles (Brazil to West Africa)
1900 miles (Howland Island to Hawaii)

Many theories try to explain Amelia's disappearance. Some believe that Earhart landed on Gardner Island, about 350 miles southeast of Howland. Small traces of evidence of someone camping on Gardner have been found. The Marshall Islands are 900 miles to the Northwest of Howland. One theory says that Amelia landed there and was captured by the Japanese because the Japanese war efforts had already begun on this island chain. There is even a theory that she finished the flight around the world, disguised herself as a normal person, changed her name, and lived incognito in New Jersey until the 1980s. Most widely believed, however, is that her plane splashed into the open ocean and sank. A small grave has been built on Howland Island to remember Amelia Earhart.

I wrestled with the idea of including this chapter. Why? I was concerned that readers may take Amelia's disappearance as a warning against creativity. Amelia was certainly creative in many ways. She leveraged publicity incredibly well. After her maintenance issue altered plans, Amelia adapted and hoped to finish the flight round-the-world on the 4th of July. Amelia would have been celebrated on a float in California that Independence Day. She was presented with the Lockheed Elektra airplane on her 39th birthday, just under a year before her disappearance. Perhaps she wanted to finish the flight before turning 40! Perhaps she was concerned about funding or the looming World War. While far from perfect, Amelia's story provides many lessons:

What got you here may not get you there.

Courage can be overdone, outpacing capability... and wisdom.

When charting a new course, you may end up at the bottom of the Pacific... or in New Jersey.

What's the ROI on inspiration?

Knowing what Amelia knew, would you do what Amelia did?

Whether you do something or nothing, there is always a price. Sometimes the risks are steep enough to justify altering plans. In Amelia's words: "Failure must be but a challenge to others."

Regina Calcaterra convinced me to include this chapter. Her book, *Etched in Sand*, is a powerful story and worth reading. On NY's Long Island, Regina's mother would frequently drive her four young kids to a new house and then disappear for weeks or months. Even when she was around, she rarely fed the kids and beat them regularly. Regina recalls being chained to a radiator and beaten with a belt. Most often, the kids were left to fend for themselves. They learned to be proficient at feeding themselves, often stealing groceries and subsisting on mac and cheese. After each move, Regina would find a library within walking distance. Unable to enroll themselves in school without an adult, Regina would spend countless hours in that library. Books brought a glimmer of hope and purpose into her own life. One of her favorite people to read about was Amelia Earhart and a favorite Earhart quotes is, "The most difficult thing is the decision to act, the rest is merely tenacity. The fears are paper tigers." Calcaterra had plenty to be afraid of and wrote, "When I'm searching for a solution or scared at night, I've begun to ask myself: *What would Amelia do?*"

Some of my favorite quotes from Amelia Earhart:

"The time to worry is three months before a flight. Decide then whether or not the goal is worth the risks involved. If it is, stop worrying. To worry is to add another hazard. It retards reactions, makes one unfit.... Hamlet would have been a bad aviator. He worried too much."

"I know a great many boys who should be making pies—and a great many girls who would be better off in manual training." (in a Barnard Athletic Association dinner speech in 1931)

"Women will gain economic justice by proving themselves in all lines of endeavor, not by having laws passed for them."

"The woman who can create her own job is the woman who will win fame and fortune."

What would Amelia do?

Involvement = Engagement

Involvement equals engagement. Or so they say. Whoever *they* are. The opposite is certainly true. Involvement facilitates, creates, or enhances engagement – and lack of involvement results in lower engagement. A friend recently described an event that we can all relate to. We see it in all types of organizations, virtually anywhere people are involved.

A married couple, we'll call them Veronica and Michael, decided to purchase new furniture. Their well-used dining room table and chairs were literally on their last legs. The couple set aside an entire Saturday to visit furniture store after furniture store. Each store had a selection of tables and chairs. The options they saw together that day ran the gamut, from inexpensive (yes, some were also cheap!) to well beyond their price range, from classic to contemporary, from simple to ornate, from sturdy to not-so-sturdy.

In the morning, they started out full of hope, anticipation, and energy. High engagement all around! After the first store, the creative juices were flowing for both Michael and Veronica. They had seen some options that they both liked and were enthusiastically bouncing ideas back and forth while driving to the next store. They walked through the second store rather briskly. Nothing caught their attention, so they headed to a third store. They were both feeling pretty good about this adventure. Both were highly engaged and excited to discuss what they thought about the options, but that was about to change.

The merchandise in the third store practically had their mouths watering. So many pieces of furniture caught their attention in this store. The prices seemed reasonable and, within a few minutes, Michael and Veronica were headed in different directions, each making note of options that had some degree of appeal for their home. After about ten minutes, the couple was back together, and both were even more excited than they had been at the start of the day. That excitement would not last.

After regrouping, they walked together through sections of the store, taking turns pointing out chair and table designs. The commentary between the couple included phrases like, "Nice!" "Oh, I like that." "These would work in our space." "What about this chair with my table – the solid dark one over there?"

Veronica was doing most of the talking, but Michael agreed with most of the options so far. Then it happened.

Michael confidently walked over to a table that he really liked. He had noticed it before, when they were separated. It was solid and built to last. He had looked over the design and thought through the common scenarios in their home. With children, art projects, dinner guests, family gatherings, and barbecues, their table would need to withstand a good beating. He did not want the legs falling off this time! Michael considered a new table to be a long-term investment and, while style mattered, functionality came first.

He put his hand on the table, smiled, and said, "How about this guy?" He tilted his head slightly to the side as he said it, expecting Veronica to really like it. To Michael, the styling, quality, and price were as perfect a combination as he had seen so far.

At first, Veronica didn't say a word. She just shook her head, made a guttural "Uggh!" sound, and her face all but screamed disgust.

Michael wasn't giving up that quickly. He walked slowly around the table and looked under it. "Hun, check this out."

She took a few steps towards the table, shook her head rapidly again, and said, "No way. Don't like it." Her nose curled in disgust, the way it always did when she was repulsed by something.

By this point, Michael was on his knees, looking under the table and anxious to show Veronica the ruggedness of this table's design. She had no interest and he only saw her back as she briskly walked over to another section of the showroom.

He was a little upset but wasn't going to give up. He took out his phone and searched for that table manufacturer. On their website, he found a variety of designs with similar structural support. Hope! He quickly caught up to Veronica and held out his phone to show her some of their other design options. She gave a very quick glance and then shut the idea down.

Michael's energy and engagement in the furniture search dropped like a lead weight. His favorite piece of furniture of the day and she didn't even give it a second look or listen as he explained what he liked about it. Michael was no longer an active furniture shopper that day.

Sure, *they* eventually picked a table and chair set, but it wasn't really *they* for the next several hours. It was Veronica, shopping with a dead weight. Michael went into the stores, discussed the options that she pointed out, and even pointed out a few more options that he thought she would like. But, for the rest of the day, Michael was not fully engaged. Not even close. He didn't really put his ideas out there. Tables or chairs that he pointed out now had just two simple criteria: 1.) he had to be quite sure that she would like the piece and 2.) if he also liked the style that was a bonus. Furniture pieces that really caught his attention were rarely mentioned because he didn't think she'd like the style. He would never find out if she did or did not like these pieces. His involvement after the brief interaction was essentially and effectively reduced to that of a wandering helper. When I speak on servant leadership, I often describe the people we choose to follow versus the people we follow because we're stuck behind them. That was Michael.

After a break for lunch, they visited a few more stores. At one store that afternoon, Michael found himself sitting in a very comfortable reclining chair with his eyes closed. She found him there and said, "We can head home. It was a good day, very productive. You're tired."

He nodded, and they walked back to the car. He wasn't tired, just bored. He wanted to be engaged but had let that interaction slow his enthusiasm down to almost nothing.

This is an interaction I've witnessed countless times in so many situations. I can appreciate the many forms of protest:
"But he shouldn't have let that comment or reaction shut him down." I agree. But he did.
"She shouldn't have been like that. My boss is exactly like that." I agree. But she was. And maybe your boss is.

The bottom line: if we want to build a culture of innovation, a culture of engagement, a culture where the best ideas are shared, we might do well to notice these little interactions and their effects, whether we're involved in the situation or not, whether we're *"Veronica"* or *"Michael."* Most of us get to play both roles, depending on the situation. Little things can create or destroy a culture, especially when we're talking about engagement and creative ideas that might not work.

If involvement equals engagement, let's make sure we, ourselves, stay involved, and let's take little actions several times each day to let others know that we want their input, that we want to hear their opinions.

Tom Peters, author of *In Search of Excellence,* shares a great concept. Four words. He recommends that leaders (and I would add parents, teachers, friends, doctors, coaches) carry a small card with them to keep score of how many times they ask a simple four word question each day. Track it in your phone every day for a week. Or just for the next hour or two. The four words: "What do you think?" The question has many versions. "What do you like about this?" "What would you change?" "What are we missing?" "What concerns you?" "What do you see that we're missing?" When

Michael was crawling under that first table, imagine if Veronica had asked:

"Michael, what do you like about the table?"

Or "Michael, what do you think matters most in this decision?"

Or "Michael, is there a price range that you're most comfortable with / or that's a little outside your comfort zone?"

If you are asking the questions but not getting answers, it may be time for a frying pan moment. In my book, *Who are you BECOMING?*, I speak in great detail about frying pan moments, moments when we get a wake-up call or reality check. Another reality check on this topic comes from the opposite angle. What if you tracked the number of times you, or even others in your organization, responded in a way that could easily be interpreted as "I'm not interested in what you think." We can say this in so many ways: emails, texts, responses that don't even acknowledge another's idea, lack of timely responses to ideas. I think the most common is also one of the simplest. Do I want to hear your current idea – or any future ideas from you? My body language, tone, or facial expression sends a message loud and clear.

You might like this simple challenge. Pick just one regular event. It could be family dinner, the car ride to take your kids to practice, a meeting that you regularly attend. It could even be an email or text conversation. During that interaction, keep track of how often you do something that could say, "I'm not that interested in your ideas." If you do this frequently, you will likely start noticing some patterns. If you don't, perhaps asking a friend to help you with it would be beneficial. Analyze these occurrences right after the interaction.

I had a meeting with a woman who's company was doing some marketing for my business. Towards the end of the meeting, she said, "Jonathan, you say that a lot." I honestly had no idea what she was referencing, but it seemed serious. "Say what a lot?"

You said, "If it's done right." That's what you say a lot.

Oh. Okay.

She continued, "My team and I get a bit paralyzed with that line. We assume that you're saying it can be done wrong, so we'd better do it right."

Ohhhh! Wow! I had no idea that this tiny phrase was having that impact. What I meant by "…if it's done right" was simply that the strategy sounded good and might take some experimentation and tweaking, but it had potential! The result of that communication was not resulting in high engagement.

Small things done well – or not so well.

I have long been a fan of Coach John Wooden and have read much about his life and leadership. If I were to try to sum up his approach in a sentence, I might say, "He majored on the majors and then majored on the minors." In other words, he figured out what mattered most and then dove into the minutia that affected those things. Little things can communicate "I value your input" and little things can communicate "I don't value your input." If building a culture of engagement and innovation matters greatly to you, is it time to make some changes?

World-Class Education for Free

Sal questioned the unquestionable, the hallowed halls and wisdom of so-called traditional education! How do we provide a free, high-quality education for anyone, anywhere in the world? Couldn't students everywhere have access to the same level of education that Bill Gates' kids have... and for free? Sal seems to have a deep appreciation for Einstein's Hour: what are the questions to ask? You'll see shortly some of the powerful questions Sal asks. But he didn't start with big questions. He failed forward. Iterated. Started with a small – yet worthwhile question.

I read a recent article that claimed, "90% of our kids are in public education, so let's fix that rather than send funds elsewhere." If we want the best possible options, wouldn't we want both? Great ideas from within and outside the current system? How often is throwing money at a massive system the catalyst for positive significant change? Recall the creativity continuum and refrigeration versions 1.0 to 2.0 to 3.0. No company made any of the major leaps. In most cases of major innovation, disruptive ideas came from outside the industry. Even if this were not the case – even if only a few occasional brilliant ideas came from outside an industry, wouldn't we want them? Don't we want the best possible ideas around educating the future of the world? Our own experiences tells us that highly creative moments often come when resources are scarce – we lack money, contacts, time, influence, resources, an office, a market, a product or service to sell, an effective way to communicate with our children, experience.

I love learning and I love spending time with people who are passionate about learning. I've spoken for and worked with education organizations around the world. The field of education has some of the world's most passionate and creative people. I don't think I am alone in wanting the best of the best teaching my kids because, as teacher turned astronaut on the tragic Challenger flight, Christa McAuliffe put it, "I touch the future. I teach."

Mark Twain once wrote, "Necessity is the mother of taking chances." Yes, *taking chances*, but in education? Did your heart rate quicken? Taking chances sounds great. Experimenting. Trying some approaches that might be slightly – or even radically – different. Excellent. *But not with my kids!* Let's take a few steps back before we tackle this emotionally charged topic.

We get excited about our children. We want what's best for them, but we also don't want what's worst... I say that because we might be tempted to make some mediocre, but predictably *not too bad*, choices for our children in order to avoid what we think might be a failure, even if the experiment has the potential to be great. We will take some chances, but they tend to be very calculated risks. Experimentation in education tends to shy away from that which could be great in either direction: great successes or great failures.

Fortunately, Sal didn't begin with a grand experiment on the entire education system. He was simply trying to help a family member. He harbored no mastermind scheme to disrupt educational institutions. Sal didn't even plan to be involved in education at all. He was simply offering his cousin, Nadia, a helping hand. The families were together over the Fourth of July and Nadia had just bombed a 7th grade math placement test. Sal compared learning certain mathematical concepts to learning to turn left on a bicycle. If you don't really get good at it, it will get you in trouble at some point! Sal accepted the challenge and that's exactly what it turned out to be. The cousins lived more than a thousand miles apart, so they communicated via phone, email, and Skype. It worked, but not very well. Finding common times to get together made it difficult. Nadia wouldn't always ask questions and Sal couldn't tell if the lessons were getting through. To alleviate the timing challenge, Sal filmed his lessons and shared them via YouTube. As an unintended side benefit, Nadia could re-watch entire lessons or segments if she didn't fully grasp a concept. She gave Sal feedback on which teaching approaches worked best and eventually told Sal that she liked him better on video than in person! Over time, Sal Khan's YouTube videos were shared with other math students. The seedling of the Khan Academy was taking root.

Sal wanted to teach the way that he wished he had been taught, to "restore the excitement" to learning. In his own words:

"I was constrained by no orthodoxy regarding the right way to do things.... I started experimenting with some ideas... they pointed to the possibility of rethinking education as we know it.... I proceeded by trial and error (yes, errors are allowed) and within the time constraints imposed by a rather demanding day job as a hedge fund analyst.... The resources available to this new entity were almost comically meager... a PC, $20 worth of screen capture software, and an $80 pen tablet... I hacked together some quizzing software.... I have always had these romantic notions of starting writing software that could help people learn, so I started writing a little tool that would give Nadia and her brothers... practice problems. I didn't trust them when they said how long it took them or whatever else. I put a database behind it and that became a useful tutorial tool because I could see where they had gaps, I could intervene appropriately, and I could give them as much practice as they needed.... Video allows you to work at your own time and pace, and you only watch the videos if you want an on-demand explanation."

Just a decade after its humble beginnings, the Khan Academy had thousands of videos and over a billion views. As I write these words in 2023, Khan Academy is used by over 135 million students and countless teachers and parents, available in about 200 countries, translated into 50 languages, and has built an incredible dashboard so that students, parents, and teachers can get a real-time and personalized assessment of progress. Which problems does a student struggle with? Which problems does a student just breeze through? Can a student who has mastered a topic help others who need support in that area? As a parent, coach, or teacher, you can even create tailored assignments for classes or individual students. Khan Academy is used to compliment or supplement classroom learning. Many parents use it for homeschooling, tutoring, or for learning about topics that interest them. Some parents simply ask that their children "play" on Khan Academy for 20 minutes before playing other video games or watching TV. I know many parents who challenge their kids to invest 3 hours on Khan Academy every week for a year to earn the privilege of getting their first car or a season pass to a ski mountain. Iterate with this one and please contact me with your ideas! Some schools use Khan Academy to help them "flip the classroom" – Khan Academy is used for teaching the lessons, freeing up classroom time for homework, labs, experiential learning and more individualized tutoring, often pairing students to teach each other. A student who excels in solving certain problems now gets the added benefit of mentoring a classmate. What an amazing way to strengthen the learning!

A first-generation college student currently attending Stanford University said, "For all the times I couldn't turn to my parents for homework help, I had Khan Academy videos to help me. Khan Academy was the private tutor that my family could not afford. For all the times I wanted to learn for the sake of learning, I would pick from the hundreds of Khan Academy videos."

A few of Sal Khan's questions:

- Is the teacher's job to teach? ... or to facilitate learning?
- Should kids have more structure or less?
- Are we testing too little or too much? Do the standardized exams measure durable learning or just a knack for taking standardized exams? What do tests really test?

- Why do students forget so much of what they have supposedly "learned" as soon as an exam has been taken?
- Why do grown-ups sense such a disconnect between what they studied in school and what they do in the real world?
- How can we provide a free, world-class education for anyone, anywhere?
- Does the traditional classroom style still make sense in a digital world?
- What if the school day were shorter? What if we didn't think high school required 4 years?
- What is the purpose of homework in the first place (before asking what type or how much is the right amount)?
- How valuable is homework that isn't reviewed?
- Does class size matter if most teaching is purely lecture?
- What matters more: student to teacher ratio or student to valuable interaction with teacher ratio? In other words, even if the student/teacher ratio is 1:1, teacher time spent grading, filing, handling administrative tasks, or just lecturing could render class size virtually irrelevant.
- Don't some aspects of learning require mastery? What if you never mastered left turns on your bicycle – or stopping? Are there similar concepts in education? How can we help ensure mastery of basics so that students don't crash later?
- Are we promoting initiative, comprehension and original thinking, or just perpetuating an empty game?

So many of Khan's questions are worth iterating or, to invent a verb, *five-percenting*! Take the question and just modify it by ~ 5%. Is a leader's job to inspire? ...or to make sure people are inspired? ...to hold people accountable? ...or ensure accountability? ...to paint and communicate the vision? ...or facilitate clarity of vision? Is a parent's job to teach character or to ensure character development? (Earlier in the book, I shared a story of my father leveraging a book by Larry Bird and Phil Jackson using a similar lever to coach Michael Jordan, Kobe Bryant, and the NBA legacy Bulls and Lakers team!) Should your company or department have more structure or less? Revisit the Coffee chapter for a unique approach to structure and framework for high engagement!

Imagine Khan Academy evolving into Pandora for learning. When you like, revisit, or skip a video, your response is used to tweak your personal learning channel. Love baseball and travelling? Your personal learning channel of math, science, literature, and history lessons is geared towards baseball and travel. The channel could increase or decrease the number of lessons based on that individual child's learning rate. For the ancient Greeks, in the age of Socrates, Plato, and Aristotle, an education tailored to the student was considered ideal. Has this really changed? I am always amused to learn about things that we "now know", as if we have suddenly and magically discovered that we put more effort into learning about things that interest us! Imagine if Google, YouTube, TikTock, Facebook, Instagram, etc. decided that their algorithm should help kids fall in love with learning and be inspired to help around the house!

Sal Khan said, "Maybe I was delusional, but I dreamed of creating something enduring and transformative, an institution for the world that could last hundreds of years and help us fundamentally rethink how schooling and might be done... I believe that the way we teach and learn is at a once-a-millennium turning point." That may be. Just over a half millennium ago, Johannes Gutenberg's printing press revolutionized the way information could be shared by chasing similar questions: is there an easier, more scalable, simpler, more cost-effective way to do this?

Can we make education both fun and highly effective? Can it be an amazing experience? Will we experiment with more strategies with the potential to be game-changers for the next generation?

Danger: Inspired Kids!

"Kids are more capable than they know."
"The freedom to fail is essential."
"It can be done bigger and bolder."

Were you nodding as you read the quotes taken from the "Tinkering School" website? When you were a child, do you recall times when you tried to do something that had never been done before (at least by you)? You succeeded. Or you failed. It was easier than you thought. Or harder. On that day, the way you saw the world, or at least some part of it, changed.

My daughters love building things with Legos. Don't get me wrong, I enjoy watching or helping them focus to finish a Lego build. But... is following the instructions the best tool for building creativity? I don't think we need a phD to answer that question.

Our safety conscious culture often pre-empts even the possibility of failure. Founder of the Tinkering School, Gever Tully said, "It is, in all manners possible to calculate, the safest time in the history of civilization to be a kid."

Just imagine sending your 6-year-old or 15-year-old to a camp that promised, "We'll build something." Sounds great! But wait, there's more. After day 1, you find out that the campers decided to build a working suspension bridge out of duct tape. Wait, there's still more! The bridge will be suspended between two trees, cross a river, and the campers will cross the bridge. Wait...! There is no design for the bridge. The kids, yours included, will "figure it out" as they go! This particular project has never been done at the camp before. Are you in?

Be honest here. Which of your family members would be slightly nervous about this camp? Perhaps the more accurate question: "which of your family members would *not* be nervous?"

And would you prefer to send *those family members* to the camp rather than your own kids?

Reflect on some of Tinkering School's past projects and keep in mind that the kids come up with the idea for the project, find materials for construction, build the project, test the project, and ultimately use the project. In the case of vehicles, they often race other teams with their finished designs.

- Hang-glider (made of PVC tubes and a tarp)
- Chariot
- Sailboat (made of cardboard and scavenged materials)
- Rail-racer (a sail-powered cart riding on railroad tracks)
- Motorcycle
- Roller coaster
- 8-person bicycle
- Suspension bridge woven from recycled grocery bags
- Drill-powered go-karts
- Rolling body suit (picture superman laying flat on the road using a suit with wheels to zoom downhill)
- Creek houses (campers slept in these houses suspended over a creek and supported by sticks lashed together)

Gever Tulley, founder of the Tinkering School, wrote a great (or scary) book, *50 Dangerous Things (you should let your children try)*. Tulley says, "When we strive to remove all risk from childhood we also remove the foundations of a rational adulthood, and we eliminate the very experiences that will help kids grow up to be the empowered, creative, brave problem-solvers that they can and must be." Here's a sampling of the 50 things:

Lick a nine-volt battery

Make the default answer "Yes!"

Play with power tools

Build a fire

Boil water in a paper cup on a gas stove

Drive a car
Cook strange things in the microwave
Make a slingshot
Be the guide on any trip (hiking, walking, biking, driving)
Explode a bottle in the freezer
Build a damn on a creek
Whittle
Make a rope swing (or something else that has to hold you up!)
Perform on the street or create a home movie

In short, tinker! Build something! Could your kids rotate your car's tires, change the oil, replace the windshield wipers, wax the car, etc.? Could they turn one of these items into a neighborhood entrepreneurial venture? Make a treehouse out of a warehouse pallet. Build a rope swing or ladder, an obstacle course, zipline, bungie swing. Design a kite that could fly behind a bicycle or one that could pull the bicycle! Make a hang glider (or parachute) for a doll, stuffed animal, or family pet. Build a cat tree or a squirrel-proof bird feeder. Create a new sport. Design a water gun obstacle course or water balloon slingshot. Build rubber band guns and create a marksmanship competition. If you don't have kids or your kids are grown, perhaps borrow some, ask a local school if you can do a tinkering project or invite a neighbor's kids over!

What if you got a group of kids together and just thought up awesome ideas over the next few days before any building started? Could be the start of a Saturday morning builder's experience. Create options. Collect options. *Five-percent* those options. Then build something, knowing that the first design probably won't work. Change the questions or resources. What can we build with just the contents of our recycling bin? What does a local plumber throw out that we could use for building? Are you preparing your kids for a future that will demand their best? Protecting and preparing are not the same thing.

"When we protect children from every possible source of danger, we also prevent them from having the kinds of experiences that develop their sense of self-reliance, their ability to assess and mitigate risk, and their sense of accomplishment." ~ Gever Tully

Gever reminds me of Amelia Earhart's dad. Perhaps we can combine Gever, Amelia, and Khan Academy to figure out the ROI of inspiration? The mind, once stretched by a new idea, never returns to its original dimensions! By the way, this doesn't just apply to kids. When an animal is hungry, it has one problem. When a human being is hungry, she has one problem. When an animal is not hungry, it has no problem. When a human being is not hungry, she has infinite problems! Tinkering School builds a healthy hunger, a healthy curiosity, a healthy belief that, "Yeah, we could build one of those!"

I have a simple challenge for you. This week (or weekend), use an idea sparked from this chapter to impact the life of someone around you. Create a meaningful memory that will last a lifetime!

Go Build Your Own School!

A teenager named Sam was fed up with high school. Shocking? It seemed that his fellow students were bored, disengaged, and learning very little. Almost all of them. To top it off, it was considered a very good high school and the disengaged students ranged from the valedictorian to the sports star to the straight-F student with dyslexia. Sam wanted learning to be fun, engaging, and purposeful. He also had the crazy notion that a high school graduate should have developed a high degree of personal responsibility and that school could assist with that process. In short, Sam wanted to change some things.

One afternoon in the beginning of a new school year, Sam let his frustrations out at the kitchen table. Sam's mother Susan said, *"Why don't you start your own school?"* In other words, instead of just complaining, *Why don't you do something about it?* Isn't that a question our culture could use much more frequently? Susan's question challenged Sam to change things, to solve the problem, to create and implement a solution. How vast the difference between complaining and building a solution! Sam could have simply muttered, "I'm bored" and left it at that. Instead, Sam happened to his schooling. He imagined alternatives and then researched, designed, proposed, refined, and launched a school within his school. He called it the *Independent Project* (or IP) and it has been running successfully for almost a decade now.

He started with questions. What do you wish you could do in your classroom but feel you're not allowed to? What engages students most? If you could change one thing about school, what would it be? If we are trying to nurture responsible individuals, why are high school students asked to take such little responsibility for their education? How can we help students to ask better questions, to take increased responsibility for their own choices? A friend of Sam's had been accepted to a one course independent study and enthusiastically exclaimed, "It's crazy. They said I can study whatever I want... I can learn *whatever* I want. How crazy is that?" High school seniors can vote, enlist in military duty, drive a car, sign six-figure college loans and decide on a career that will affect every single aspect of life. Life-altering responsibility, yet Sam's friend described it as *crazy* to be allowed to decide what to learn in just ONE class for a single semester. Crazy, indeed! Almost every minute of high school is scheduled and supervised, then we wonder why many college students' primary decision criteria for selecting classes is time of day: "No 8 am classes for me. And no Fridays!"

As Sam refined his idea, he pitched the IP to the school board. Naturally, they had questions and Sam had to refine his proposal several times before finally acquiring permission to run his school-within-a-school for half of the school year. Ask more questions about more things from more angles and with *more persistence!* The IP has three components: Academics, Individual Endeavor, and Collective Endeavor.

Academics:

Students spend the first half of each day on academics. On Monday mornings, each student selects an academic question that he is actually interest in understanding. There is a framework around the questions. For example, sometimes the questions all must be related to math. Students have asked:

- Why do wings generate lift?
- Why does it rain?
- How does sleep deprivation affect teenagers?
- What is particle physics? What is the Higgs Boson?
- Is barefoot running beneficial?
- What is the math behind poker? (one student disliked math but really liked poker!)
- What are the ramifications of oil spills in the ocean?
- How do symbiotic relationships work?

- What are the properties of fire?
- How do neon lights work? What determines their color?
- Can we make water?
- How is surface tension created?
- What are eyes made of and how do they function?
- What are alternate forms of fuel?
- How do nuclear bombs work?
- Do plant cells differ at the bottom vs. top of a mountain?
- Why we do we cry?
- How is ice cream made?
- What are the physics of skateboarding?

On Friday, each student will teach her peers about the journey and what was learned. As a part of academics, students also rotate in selecting a novel for the whole class to read every week. Books are also discussed on Fridays, often with a facilitator that might be a teacher, local college professor, or an adult from the community. The wide range of student-selected novels have included *Crime and Punishment*, *Charlotte's Web*, *As I Lay Dying*, and *Einstein's Dreams*. Students also compose their own writing related to the book of the week. Writings might be a back-story for one of the novel's characters, an alternate ending, or even a poem or short story inspired by the novel.

Individual Endeavor:

Afternoons are spent on personalized projects selected by the students. Individual Endeavors have included:
- write a novel / play
- master a musical instrument and perform a concert to demonstrate mastery
- learn culinary arts, prepare five-course meal for 80 people
- in depth study of women's trauma recovery
- build a kayak

- Western vs. Eastern medical treatment of Lyme disease

Collective Endeavor:

Afternoons for the last third of the semester are dedicated to a group project, called a Collective Endeavor. The students select a project that must be challenging enough to demand full participation for about three weeks and must serve a need outside of the school. Collective Endeavors have included putting on a play and producing a film documentary.

I highly recommend reading *A School of Our Own*, by Sam Levin and his mother, Susan Engel, as well as watching the documentary about the Independent Project online. Sam said, "Unfortunately, the things that matter most - things like being curious, being able to master something, having drive - are the hardest things to measure."

How often in your life does a frustration lead to innovation? Imagine if Sam just ignored his frustration, or wasn't quite frustrated enough to do something about it? In a recent keynote, I was speaking on clarity and mentioned the clarity of building a world-class marriage, no matter what. Several attendees approached me afterwards and thought this was a unique perspective. When I asked what made it a unique perspective, they said that the whole idea was unique, but especially the "no matter what" *clause*. I say clause because we often pursue great questions with unwritten clauses. For example, I'd love to build a world-class marriage... as long as he/she does _____. Or: how can education be incredibly engaging... as long as the teachers/local school board/DOE are the ones who make it happen.

Let's iterate Sam's mother's question: "Why don't you..." - build a school, create a program, build a world-class marriage, make college free for one person in your neighborhood, end hunger in your town, etc?

Why don't you _____?

Can't is a Silly Word

Be careful! You may say you want creativity, but are you sure? Do you, really?

Tony Hsieh, who built Zappos, the billion-dollar online shoe store famous for culture, said, "For a person, character is destiny. For a company, culture is destiny." Aren't these sentences saying the same thing? Culture is essentially the combined character of the people in a company, organization, or family. Character and culture are daily habits, whether pertaining to individuals or the group.

To build a family culture that nurtures creativity, many years ago I decided to reduce the use of words like *can't* and *impossible*. Most children hear these words 15- to 30- times more often than *can* or *possible*. There are certainly times and situations where *can't* is appropriate, but they are much less frequent than our usage of the word. With young daughters, it didn't take long to come up with a catch-phrase: *"Can't is a silly word!"* Since building character or culture is not a one-stop process, we've repeated that phrase hundreds and hundreds of times. For well over a year, it was a very intentional process. Isn't that always the case when you're trying to build a new habit, character trait, or culture? Good habits are hard to build and easy to live with. Bad habits are easy to build and hard to live with.

My youngest daughter, Maya, when she was just three- or four-years-old might say, "I can't reach the milk." I would respond, "Can't is a silly word." Maya would look at me and repeat her words with more volume, "I can't reach the milk." I would respond with, "Can't?" and then Ella, my oldest daughter and I would both say, "Can't is a silly word." A classic wonderful parenting conversation! To be honest, not all of our attempts went well. But... the continued effort to question this "can't" and "impossible" assumption we all seem to make has slowly paid off. I don't remember Maya ever responding to a collective effort like the one I've just described with, "Why thank you, Father! I must have forgotten that using 'can't' can be highly effective at shutting down my creative mind. How can I thank you enough, Dad?" Many times, Maya's response to a similar situation was quite the opposite! Either way, the conversation would continue…

Me: "Maya, how could you reach the milk?"

Maya: "I already told you, I CAN'T!"

Me: "If you used a chair, could you?"

Maya: *no response*

Me: "What if I help? Could you and I reach the milk together?"

Maya: *no response*

Me: *wondering if I should keep going… Who said building culture or building character in kids was easy?* "If we work together, do you think we could figure out how you could reach the milk?"

Maya: *with a stubborn look, opens the freezer door (our freezer is on the bottom) and climbs on the door and freezer shelf. She gets the milk, pours some, and puts it back – on a lower shelf. Her facial expression shows that she is pleased with her solution, but maybe not so pleased with my involvement in the process.*

Me: "Awesome! I knew you'd figure it out!" – *and thankful that the door didn't break in the process (yet)!*

Be careful what you wish for! Fast forward a few years and dozens of similar interactions (some handled better, some handled worse by both Dad and daughter). One morning, just before my oldest daughter turned 11, she let me know that she can do whatever she wants. Without really thinking about it, I offhandedly replied, "No, I don't think that's really true." Her response, "Yeah, it is."

What's that nonchalant robotic reply passed down for millennia from parent to child? "No. Not while you live in my house."

Ella continued: "Hmmm. But I can do whatever I want."

I thought she was kidding and said, "No. You can't do anything you want."

She said, "Really? Give me an example of something I can't do."

I said, "I could give you plenty. Like leaving your bike out in the rain for a week. You can't do that."

At this point, Maya was walking by and with a quick smile, looked at me and Ella and practically sang, "Can't is a silly word. Ella can leave her bike out in the rain for a week. She actually did."

True enough. She could and did! It's very important to note that many things that can be done (or attempted) are not good choices. Leaving the bike out would not show responsibility or good character. Shouldn't and can't have different meanings.

While my daughters and I were just kidding around in the above conversation, I hope you see the point about culture. If you want a culture that questions things, that values ideas from many sources, that assumes there are many solutions, that celebrates the lessons that often only come from failure, get ready!

Are you sure that you want to build a more creative culture? Creative people change things. They question things. I'm not naïve enough to think I'm the first to arrive at the conclusion that a lack of creativity is more predictable and a lot easier to manage! Why do you think most big budget movies lately are franchises? Star Wars Episode 34. Frozen 3. Spiderman 6? Walt Disney's brother, Roy, was the finance guy. He kept trying to convince Walt to make version 2 of cartoons and films. Walt had no interest. He understood the financial predictability, but wanted to create things that didn't yet exist. Creative people change things. They can and they do. Can't is a silly word.

Entrepreneur Adventure

It is possible. The teenagers just looked at me with a sense of confusion. Teachers and chaperones accompanying the Future Business Leaders of America event also looked confused. After delivering their opening keynote, I was facilitating a short workshop on marketing for start-up businesses. Perhaps they were wondering what my challenge had to do with marketing, or business at all, for that matter.

"Lift the instructor 6 inches off the ground for 1 minute."

The directions were simple and clear, but six student volunteers looked at me and at each other in disbelief as the seconds ticked by. Within moments, a few of the volunteers seemed to realize that this was the actual challenge. For six strong teenagers working together – I had asked for six strong volunteers – lifting an adult instructor 6 inches off the ground for a minute shouldn't be that difficult. One volunteer proposed that I lay flat on the floor, so they could lift a horizontal body. This proposal gathered acceptance with the other lifters, but now it was my turn to have a look of disbelief! I slowly accepted the idea that I had just subjected myself to being lifted half a foot above a concrete floor – while lying flat on my back. The scenario was about to unfold when the strongest volunteer stepped forward abruptly and picked me up by himself. I was about eighteen inches off the ground and the lifter was exerting significant effort. I am six foot four and probably not the easiest person to lift. After 60 seconds, the workshop attendees burst into applause. Expressions changes from a look of success back to a look that said, "Why did we do that?"

I wasn't ready to answer that question just yet. Instead, I asked for just one volunteer who would not be physically capable of lifting me alone. A petite young lady was volunteered by her friends. As she walked to the front of the room, the rest of the attendees let out a collective sigh of "No way!"

The *volunteer* looked at me but didn't say anything. Nor did she return to her seat. As she stood in front of her peers, we could see her mind working though the challenge. She read the instruction slowly aloud and looked at me inquisitively. "Is that it?"

Me: "Yes."

Volunteer: "Are there any other rules?"

Me: "I don't see any."

"Hmmm" was all she replied. The seconds ticked by. Suddenly, her face lit up.

She asked one of the students in the front row to please stand up. Then she took that student's chair and put it in front of me. She was now standing in front of the room with her arms folded and a proud look of accomplishment across her face.

"Mr. Fanning, would you please stand on the chair?"

I followed her request and she calmly started the timer. Her minute was a lot easier on both the "lifter" and "lifted"!

When my feet were once again planted on the floor, I asked the students what this young lady had done. Many answers came. "She cheated." "She used a chair." "She found resources." "She worked smarter, not harder." "She engaged her mind, not just muscle."

I changed the question. "I'm looking for a one word answer."

"Chair?"

"Think?"

"Smarter?"

"Succeed?"

I finally heard the word I was looking for: "Leverage." Yes, *leverage*! If there is one word that a startup entrepreneur needs to understand, this is probably it. At least it's on the shortlist. I then asked the group what this young lady had leveraged. They took a few minutes, but came up with a good list: her mind, ideas, a chair, me, other people's efforts, the environment around her, knowledge, language, relationships, persuasion, communication, resources.

"What else could be leveraged to accomplish our goal?" I had barely finished asking the question when hands went up around the room: Other chairs, furniture of any kind, that stack of books on the desk, other people in the room... I repeated this phrase with emphasis on *"in the room?"*

Oh yeah, other people not in the room, resources not in the room, ideas from other people not in the room!

At this point, I showed the group two pictures. The first was of a man standing next to a wall. He was standing on a stack of ladders that were just piled up, none of them standing up for proper use. The caption under the picture read, "It doesn't matter how many resources you have... if you don't know how to use them." The second picture was a black and white photo of a man in a bowler hat. Andrew Carnegie. Carnegie was the wealthiest person in the world at the beginning of the 20th century. As a young man, he wrote a simple and clear note to himself that was found in one of his desk drawers after his death. The note read: "I will spend the first half of my life earning a fortune and the second half of my life giving it all away." That is precisely what he did. Upon his death, Carnegie had given away all but about 6% of his net worth. One of the most visible beneficiaries is the library system. Carnegie funded the start of 2,509 libraries across the United States. Carnegie famously said, "I would rather have one percent of 100 people's efforts than 100 percent of my own." He also said, "The way to become rich is to put all your eggs in one basket and then watch that basket." Many of us today seem to take precisely the opposite advice, "Diversify your investment (and then you don't have to watch it)." With my speaking schedule, I meet aspiring entrepreneurs on a weekly basis. I often find myself explaining that having money to start your business is often perceived as an advantage, but it often is not. As Malcolm Gladwell wisely describes in his best-selling book, ***David*** *and Goliath*, "There is a set of advantages that have to do with material resources, and there is a set that have to do with the absence of material resources..." Quite often, perceived disadvantages are turned into advantages. For example, a young girl in one of my recent Entrepreneur Adventure workshops informed me that she was dyslexic. I said, "Excellent! About 40% of all self-made millionaires are dyslexic." Not the answer she or her mother expected. Lacking financing, connections, resources, can be turned into incredibly creative solutions (or leverage for you to seek out those creative solutions). Carnegie was poor and worked to feed his family from the age of 12. He missed out on most formal education, so he spent significant time with books. This "disadvantage" became emotional leverage to fuel his desire to provide others with access to books. In fact, Carnegie said, "I choose free libraries as the best agencies for improving the masses of the people because they give nothing for nothing. They only help those who help themselves." Carnegie understood leverage. One of his libraries is just a half mile from my house. In fact, some of this book was written on the top floor of that Carnegie funded library.

Pay attention to leverage over the next few days. Notice it in various forms.

If you take a few minutes, you can probably list dozens of good questions that incorporate leverage. A friend of mine had lunch with a billionaire and was given a unique perspective. The billionaire said that he liked to be paid three times for every business venture. First while he was building the business, second once the business was operating without his involvement, and third when he sold the business. That approach just incorporates a simple question of leverage. How can I get paid more than once for every effort? Or how can I use every bit of work more than once? How can I answer this question once, instead of a few dozen times?

Rate yourself, 1 to 10. How well do you currently use leverage? What will you change?

Who Doesn't Want a Free Boat?

I would like to have a boat. Who doesn't? I love to joke with friends that I *need* a boat. Of course, I do not *need* a boat. Part of the point to the joke is to point out how our choice of language often distorts or exaggerates reality. On the soccer teams that I coach, the girls will tell me they are dying of thirst, or that they need a rest. They're exhausted. Then they'll sprint off the field or over to tell a parent or grandparent some important message. Better yet, parents at the end of a season will bring donuts to the game and the exhausted kids will sprint to get first choice. I am not sure when parents decided donuts were a good idea after a soccer game. I must have missed something. Back to needing a boat.

We were heading to Ocean City, Maryland, to spend several days at the beach with some family members. As per Einstein's "55 minutes figuring out what questions to ask", I like to spend some time mapping out a few questions before family trips and holidays. The trip would be fun. We'd have both quality and quantity time together. But, what could we do to make it a life-changing experience? How could this trip be more than just fun, but a learning experience that would help shape the way my daughters see the world? What could we do so that learning would engage their minds in such a way that they would want to participate – where the lesson would be so engaging that they would invite their friends or cousins to participate?

These are just some of the questions I was exploring before the trip. An idea popped into my head about a boat. After all, we've already established that I do need one. During the five-hour drive to Ocean City, I talked with my daughters about the idea of having a boat. We talked about where we'd use it, who we'd invite, what kinds of trips we'd take, what food we'd pack for longer excursions. We even imagined that we might be towing it along on this trip. We looked at maps and planned all sorts of trips that our boat could take. Naturally, we passed many boats on our journey and it became a game: "Look! That's the boat we need!"

But then we changed the conversation slightly to "how?" Could my daughters, who were then in 6th and 2nd grades buy their daddy a boat? They decided that they could. It would be my present for the next ten years, covering every birthday, Christmas, Father's Day, etc. for a decade. We changed the question again. How can we get a boat without spending any money? How can we use a boat for free? How could we have access to a boat with Other People's Money (OPM)? How could we enjoy the fun side of boating without the headache side (maintenance, storage, expenses, etc.)? We decided that we would collect ideas, options. It was so much fun and we even invited some friends and family who were not with us to participate.

Here is a partial list of our ideas:
- tours
- fireworks
- timeshare
- rental
- fishing trips
- we do maintenance on someone else's boat in exchange for use
- dinner cruises
- do odd jobs for people who have a boat in exchange for use
- raffle tickets
- dinner and theater combos where we are the transportation
- marriage proposal vehicle
- wedding photos on the boat
- scuba tours
- educational programs
- field trips
- boater safety lessons
- charge for tubing rides
- water skiing lessons

- water sports camps (in summer, after school, linked to a camp)
- someone else buys boat and we give them something in exchange, like a week in Charleston, hotel points, frequent flyer miles
- it's someone else's boat all together, and we make an arrangement to use it (we could wash it, fill it with gas, transport it for them)
- package with dinner on the other side of the river, tours of Hudson River towns, work with realtors, new Tappan Zee Bridge tours, bridges of NYC tours, West Point tours
- prepay for your day/week
- lottery... 1 dollar for a chance to... or $10 for chance to... get a free day or week on the boat (link to tubing day? Trip to statue of liberty? Etc)
- Nantucket tours, whaling, dolphin swim, seal watching
- rent on boatsetter, craigslist, or other websites
- rent as package with a local Airbnb or local restaurant
- signs (advertise along beaches)
- daring trip, get sponsors
- find a boat you really like, and then arrange to do all the maintenance on it (or wash & wax it) in trade for a certain number of days using it
- buy classic boats that will go up and value, and acquire investors for them
- arrange with a boat dealer to do demos for them
- arrange with people who want to sell their used boat to do demos or to keep it in working order
- arrange with the boat rental place to do demos for them, for every customer you have them, you get credit for some amount of time on the boat
- work for a boat rental place
- work for boat dealership
- work for person who owns boat

- work for a marina
- GoFundMe
- get your whole family involved in buying a boat and you manage it
- same with several families or organizations (church, rotary, condo association, etc)
- 30 families invest $1000 each, each gets 5 days on boat/year
- similar, but you get a full day per $300 or 5 days for 1000.
- similar, but you get a day every single year for 10 years for $2,000
- partner w/ very expensive schools, colleges, private schools and NY tours for their VIP's.
- Same with corporate events
- same with entertaining children of corporate events visiting
- similar with visitor children entertainment for the day.
- Birthday parties
- raffle around 1 thing (4th of July fireworks @ Westpoint?)
- Pay $300/yr & get it on your child's birthday every single year or a rain date
- prepay 250 for a future date (get ~50 people)
- Hudson Valley tourism / sponsor
- winery tour
- hotel tour
- haunted house tour
- historic sites tour, battle fields, Henry Hudson's voyage
- real estate tours
- partner with professional sports teams, NFL, NBA, MLB, soccer. (for example San Antonio Riverwalk, San Francisco Bay Manhattan with the Yankees or Mets, subway series, Jets, Giants, Knicks, Nets, Rangers, Islanders)
- get the manufacturer to give one, in exchange for documenting adventures socially for a period of time.

- get sponsors to pay for it, advertise on outside of boat + socially mentions during adventures.
- pay for it, but rent it out until it's fully paid back
- make a deal to sell 3 boats, and get one for free.

I bet that you can add at least 5 of your own ideas to this list. As you can see, many of the ideas are just versions of others. We certainly used the "Build-build-build-build-Jump" approach. Once we had an idea, we made many iterations of that idea, sometimes combining several ideas in the process. We didn't worry about repetition or the quality of the ideas. We changed the question several times in order to find different answers. For example, we asked, "If the funding had to all come from 1 person, how could we do it?" and "If the 'other people' were only going to contribute a dollar or two, how could we make that work?" Practice collecting ideas, perspectives, experiences... options! Practice changing your questions. Will someone use one of these ideas, or several in combination, to get a free boat? I expect someone will. Try a similar exercise with a weekend getaway, a trip to Europe, a motorcycle tour of the National Parks in California, a dream vacation at Disney, marketing or financial services for your start-up business, renovating your house, taking your spouse out for an amazing dinner, etc! For over a decade, my wife and I have been asking – no pursuing – the question: "How can we spend a month every year in Europe. We didn't ask the question just once or twice. We chase it. And we've been blessed to spend several months in Italy, a month in the UK, a month in Germany, several months in Poland. The quality of our lives hinges on the quality of the questions we pursue!

Why Wrights Were 1ˢᵗ in Flight!

Why? Yes, the Wright Brothers had a compelling *Why*. When I gave my first TEDx talk, Simon Sinek was scheduled to speak right after me. He is well-known for his book and TED Talk, *Start with Why*, and I was looking forward to discussing this with him. I love the concept of Why. Throughout history, people who are passionate about their *Why* tend to change things. But having a strong *Why* is not why the Wright Brothers were the first to fly! (I almost took that sentence out, but my daughters convinced me that you would appreciate the rhyme.)

Virtually everyone involved in flying experiments had a significant *Why*. Da Vinci. Lilienthal. Chanute. Cayley. Pénaud. Montgomery. Pilcher. Weißkopf. Bell. Langley. Think about it. Passion for flying – is that really rare? Throughout history, millions (or probably billions) of people have stared up in awe of a hawk soaring through the sky. The passion – the Why – was there.

What truly separated the Wrights? A combination of the 5 pillars in this book. For example, they pursued some very different questions. Einstein's Hour: 55 minutes to determine the questions / 5 minutes to ask and answer the questions. The Wrights invested considerable time determining the real problems to be solved. You may be thinking, "How do we fly, is the question, right?" Wrong! A few of the questions the Wrights pursued:

1. How can we:
    a. Experiment & Fail (a lot)
    b. Learn (a lot)
    c. And Stay Alive
2. What is the problem to be solved? Is it:
    a. Propulsion
    b. Lift
    c. Yaw (steering like a car, but in the air)

    d. Equilibrium (balance, like leaning on a bicycle)

The questions summarized in part 1 above might be the most important lesson from the Wrights. They essentially asked, how can we experiment, fail, learn, and stay alive. More succinctly: "How do we learn without dying?" While pursuing the questions outlined under part 2, the Wrights realized that the problem to be solved was equilibrium – or balance – in the air.

In 1900, before the Wright's first glider was even assembled, Wilbur wrote a letter to Octave Chanute verifying that these were the two problems that they would pursue:

"As to his [Lilienthal's] method, the fact that in five years' time he spent only about five hours, altogether, in actual flight is sufficient to show that his method was inadequate. Even the simplest intellectual or acrobatic feats could never be learned with so short practice..."

[How do we learn without dying? How do we get a significant amount of time in the air while staying alive? Less than 4 years before Wilbur's letter, Lilienthal died in a glider accident near Berlin. His last words: "Opfer müssen gebracht werden!" (*Sacrifices must be made!*) The Wrights very deliberately chose a strategy where the ultimate *Opfern* (sacrifice) – death – was highly unlikely.]

"My observation of the flight of buzzards leads me to believe that they regain their lateral balance when partly overturned by a gust of wind, by a torsion of the tips of the wings. If the rear edge of the right wing tip is twisted upward and the left downward the bird becomes an animated windmill sand instantly begins to turn, a line from its head to its tail being the axis."

[Balance is the problem to be solved. How will we accomplish equilibrium in the air? What lessons can we learn safely from observing birds?]

The Wrights spent hundreds of hours staring up into the heavens, awed by the mystery of flight. For millennia, flying creatures have captured the imagination of humanity. Observing a hawk in flight is fascinating. In one of my books (*Who are you BECOMING?*), I shared the story of learning to hang glide at Kitty Hawk. Flying is a great adventure, but a gigantic gap exists between wondering, "What must it be like to soar like a bird?" and trying to build a machine that makes it possible. While wondering has occupied countless members of our species, attempting to bridge that gap has not been as common an endeavor.

When Orville and Wilbur were just seven- and eleven-years-old, their father, Bishop Milton Wright, brought a flying toy back from one of his church trips. Milton often brought gifts for his boys that would engage their imaginations – including fossils, interesting rocks, and mechanical toys. Milton also allowed his sons to miss school on occasion to pursue their own intellectual interests.

In describing their childhood, Orville once said, "We were lucky enough to grow up in a home environment where there was always much encouragement to children to pursue intellectual interests; to investigate whatever aroused their curiosity."

This toy "flying bat" was a rubber band-powered helicopter designed by the French inventor, Alphonse Pénaud. Years later, the brothers would study Pénaud's aeronautics work in depth. The boys played with that fragile toy until it wore out and then built their own versions of the bat. When they built a copy that was twice as tall, they learned (without dying) that flight of an object twice as long needed more than double the lift power. Years later, they would calculate that this craft would require eight times the lift power.

As the Wright's passionate interest in flying grew, they invested countless hours in bird-watching. Then, in 1899, Wilbur wrote to the Smithsonian:

I have been interested in the problem of mechanical and human flight ever since as a boy I constructed a number of bats of various sizes after the style of Cayley's and Penaud's machines. My observations since have only convinced me more firmly that human flight is possible and practicable. It is only a question of knowledge and skill just as in all acrobatic feats. Birds are the most perfectly trained gymnasts in the world and are specially well fitted for their work, and it may be that man will never equal them, but no one who has watched a bird chasing an insect or another bird can doubt that feats are preformed which require three or four times the effort required in ordinary flight. I believe that simple flight at least is possible to man and that the experiments and investigations of a large number of independent workers will result in the accumulation of information and knowledge and skill which will finally lead to accomplished flight.

.... I am about to begin a systematic study of the subject in preparation for practical work to which I expect to devote what time I can spare from my regular business. I wish to obtain such papers as the Smithsonian Institution has published on this subject, and if possible a list of other works in print in the English language.... I wish to avail myself of all that is already known and then if possible add my mite to help on the future workers who will attain final success. I do not know the terms on which you send out your publications but if you will inform me of the cost I will remit the price.

After reading everything they could find related to manned flight, the brothers decided that their own glider experiments should be conducted in Kitty Hawk. Wilbur explained the reasons via letters to their father in September of 1900. (underline and bold added for my emphasis)

"The wind there [Kittyhawk] is stronger than any place near home and is almost constant, so that it is not necessary to wait days or weeks for a suitable breeze. It is much cheaper to go to a distant point where practice may be constant than to choose a nearer spot where three days out of four might be wasted. **_My idea is merely to experiment and practice with a view to solving the problem of equilibrium._** *I have plans which I hope to find much in advance of the methods tried by previous experimenters. When once a machine is under proper control under all conditions, the motor problem will be quickly solved. A failure of motor will then simply mean a slow descent and safe landing instead of a disastrous fall.* **_In my experiments I do not expect to rise many feet from the ground, and in case I am upset there is nothing but soft sand to strike on._** *I do not intend to take dangerous chances, both because I have no wish to get hurt and because a fall would stop my experimenting, which I would not like at all.* **_The man who wishes to keep at the problem long enough to really learn anything positively cannot take dangerous risks._** *Carelessness and overconfidence are usually more dangerous than deliberately accepted risks. I am constructing my machine to sustain about five times my weight and am testing every piece. I think there is no possible chance of its breaking while in the air. If it is broken it will be by awkward landing.*

My machine will be trussed like a bridge and will be much stronger than that of Lilienthal, which, by the way, was upset through the failure of a movable tail and not by breakage of the machine. The tail of my machine is fixed, and even if my steering arrangement should fail, it would still leave me with the same control that Lilienthal had at best. My machine is more simple in construction and at the same time capable of greater adjustment and control than previous machines.

I have not taken up the problem with the expectation of financial profit. Neither do I have any strong expectation of achieving the solution at the present time or possibly any time. My trip would be no great disappointment if I accomplished practically nothing.

Let's take a look at a brief timeline of the Wright's experiments:

1899 (Dayton) – the brothers built a 6-foot-wide kite and experimented with it in around Dayton. From their extensive study of birds in flight and reading everything they could get their hands on related to flight, they decided that control should be done by "wing-warping." While talking with a bike shop customer in July, Wilbur picked up a cardboard box that once held a bicycle inner tube and began bending it back and forth. Suddenly, he realized that he could warp the kite's wings in a similar manner.

1900 (October, Kitty Hawk) – about a dozen glides with Wilbur piloting Glider 1

1901 (July & August, Kitty Hawk) – Glider 2, larger wings: 50-100 flights and many just as a kite tethered. Glider did NOT perform very well. Lift and drag measurements made the brothers conclude that the prevailing data (Lilienthal's tables) were not accurate. According to the Lilienthal tables, the 1901 glider should have created 3 times the lift that it actually created. The brothers were willing to question one of their own aviation heroes.

Orville Wright: "If we all worked on the assumption that what is accepted as true is really true, then there would be little hope for advance."

1901 (September 18, Chicago) – Octave Chanute invited Wilbur to speak to the Western Society of Engineers. Just minutes into the talk, Wilbur announced that it could take all evening to describe how birds are able to fly. Instead, he held a sheet of paper horizontally and then allowed it to flutter to the ground, saying (again, bold underlines are not Wilbur's, added for my emphasis):

*If I take this piece of paper, and after placing it parallel with the ground, quickly let it fall, it will not settle steadily down as a staid, sensible piece of paper ought to do, but it insists on contravening every recognized rule of decorum, turning over and darting hither and thither in the most erratic manner, much after the style of an **untrained horse**. Yet this is the style of steed that men must learn to manage before flying can become an everyday sport. The bird has learned this art of equilibrium, and learned it so thoroughly that its skill is not apparent to our sight. We only learn to appreciate it when we try to imitate it. Now, **there are two ways of learning to ride a fractious horse: One is to get on him and learn by actual practice how each motion and trick may be best met; the other is to sit on a fence and watch the beast a while, and then retire to the house and at leisure figure out the best way of overcoming his jumps and kicks.** The latter system is the safest, but the former, on the whole, turns out the larger proportion of good riders. **It is very much the same in learning to ride a flying machine; if you are looking for perfect safety, you will do well to sit on a fence and watch the birds; but if you really wish to learn, you must mount a machine and become acquainted with its tricks by actual trial.***

*Herr Otto Lilienthal seems to have been the first man who really comprehended that **balancing was the first instead of the last of the great problems in connection with human*** *__flight__. He began where others left off, and thus saved the many thousands of dollars that it had theretofore been customary to spend in building and fitting expensive engines to machines which were uncontrollable when tried. He built a pair of wings of a size suitable to sustain his own weight, and made use of gravity as his motor. This motor not only cost him nothing to begin with, but it required no expensive fuel while in operation, and never had to be sent to the shop for repairs. It had one serious drawback, however, in that it always insisted on fixing the conditions under which it would work. These were, that the man should first betake himself and machine to the top of a hill and fly with a downward as well as a forward motion. Unless these conditions were complied with, gravity served no better than a balky horse -- it would not work at all. Although Lilienthal must have thought the conditions were rather hard, he nevertheless accepted them till something better should turn up; and in this manner __he made some two thousand flights__, in a few cases landing at a point more than 1,000 feet distant from his place of starting. Other men, no doubt, long before had thought of trying such a plan. __Lilienthal not only thought, but acted; and in so doing probably made the greatest contribution to the solution of the flying problem that has ever been made by any one man.__*

1901-'02 (Winter, Dayton) – The brothers continued their experimentation back in Ohio, testing model wings attached to a bicycle wheel that they mounted to the handlebars of a bicycle and rode through the streets. They also designed and built a wind tunnel and created their own lift tables.

1902 (Sept 19 – Oct 24, Kitty Hawk) – Glider 3, designed over the previous winter with all new data from wind tunnel experiments.

Conducted about 1,000 glides. Glider gave the pilot full control over the three dimensions of flight (pitch, yaw, and roll).

1902-'03 (Winter, Dayton) – After an extensive search for a powerful, yet light-weight motor, the brothers decided to build their own motor, thus providing propulsion for their planned powered flight attempts.

1903 (Kitty Hawk) – Glider 4 conducted another 200 glides while the brothers built motorized Flyer 1. December 17th, 1903 at 10:35am – first powered flight by Wilbur. 12 seconds. Second and third powered flights follow shortly afterwards that same morning.

The Wrights pursued a dramatically different set of questions as compared with their contemporaries. What is the real problem to be solved? How do we experiment a lot, crash a lot, yet live and learn? What assumptions or measurements might be wrong? A significant portion of their experimentation occurred with kites, in wind tunnels, or with a glider that was flying over soft sand very close to the ground. Did they fail? In the attempt to fly, they failed more than anyone in history. The Wrights were world-class innovators because they pursued better questions and developed strategies to survive more failures than any aeronautical pioneer in history.

Face First in the Snow

"The desire for safety stands against every great and noble enterprise." ~Tacitus (first century Roman senator and historian)

Most of us, at times, take the desire for safety well beyond safety, all the way to a desire for comfort, or even a desire to avoid anything that might be remotely uncomfortable.

My oldest daughter, Ella, learned to ski a few years ago and handed me a remarkable lesson. Over the course of several visits to a ski mountain, we spent time on the bunny slope and then on some of the beginner slopes. Ella loved it, and even the colder temperatures didn't bother her. On an absolutely beautiful afternoon, we ratcheted it up a notch and tried some of the intermediate slopes. Then, on one of the lift rides, she noticed a racing course and heard the announcer calling out the times of each finisher. It wasn't the most serious race course, but it did have gates and a few relatively steep sections.

"Can we do that?" she said to me, pointing to the course from the ski lift.

"Sure." I watched a few of the racers and knew that they were going significantly faster than Ella had ever skied.

The first run went well. My eight-year-old daughter wasn't the fastest skier through the course. In fact, when they announced her time, I think it was about three to four times longer than most of the other skiers. She didn't try to go fast, but did go on the correct side of each gate.

As we stood just past the finish line, my daughter looked up at me and was absolutely beaming.

"How'd I do?" she asked.

We stood there watching the next few skiers and heard their times announced. Ella face showed that she was trying to figure out how her time compared with the other racers.

"Am I winning, Daddy?" Her face was full of hope and expectancy.

I had to tell her the truth. "It looks like they're faster than you were on that first run."

She didn't look disappointed at all. Instead, she said, "Can we go again?"

"Sure. Let's go!"

On the lift ride up this time, she evaluated each of the racers and listened to each time as they were called out.

Near the top, Ella announced, "This time I'm going to go so fast." Her head was nodding and she was staring straight ahead with her teeth clenched.

"Okay!" I thought it would turn out just fine.

At the top of the slope, we got off the ski lift and turned towards the trail with the race course for a second attempt. On this run, Ella would be the fastest of anyone whose time she had heard. Of this, she seemed quite convinced!

We skied our way to the beginning of the race course and Ella took her position in the starting gate. By this point, she even had a racer number, so she could see her position on the ski mountain's race website. Exciting stuff. This was going to be big!

Three, two, one, and she was off. The beginning of the course was not very steep, and Ella made the first few turns very smoothly. She was gaining speed and did nothing to intentionally slow herself down. She was serious about this run!

The trail became significantly steeper a few hundred yards into the run and I was skiing on the open side of the trail, alongside the race course. I was filming my racing girl and my emotions were mixed as her speed continued to increase. This was incredible, but she was now going about as fast as she ever had. Would she do anything to slow down?

That question answered itself almost as soon as I had the thought. No. She was flying down the slope and, up until this point, had made every turn.

I can ski, but trying to film at this speed was a bit challenging. I had to keep up, though, because I was sure this was one of those special moments. I knew Ella would want to see her record-breaking race and I could imagine her excitement in sharing it with friends and family, especially her many cousins.

About half way through the course, there was a flatter section with wide sweeping turns. Ella handled this with ease and I made a few quick turns to slow my pace and stay in control. Just after the flat section came the steepest part of the course. Ella attacked the challenge and within seconds, I could see where this was going.

She made the first gate in the steep section, then the second. But as she turned out of the second gate, I could see her whole body start to wobble. Her skis began to separate a little too far and then one ski went up in the air as her whole body shifted forward and to one side. She was at her top speed and heading straight towards one of the gates with absolutely no control. A crash was eminent.

I was about fifty yards away, skiing parallel to the course and still filming. (The video for this chapter is worth checking out...) Thoughts of rescuing Ella from this crash rushed through my mind, but I knew it just wasn't possible. She would go down and there was nothing I could do to stop the fall. I even had a fleeting thought to quickly stop the video, knowing that Ella's mom – my wife, Dominika – might not be as excited as Ella and I were about this attempt at a ski record. As soon as I had that thought, I ignored it, knowing that I could edit the crash out of the video later. I had already turned towards Ella as her body tumbled forward. Faceplant! My little girl went face first into the snow, skidded, flipped, and rolled to a stop a few dozen yards further down the slope.

By the time she stopped sliding, I was right next to her. I wasn't sure how she would respond, but knew how contagious parents' responses often are, so despite my worries, I worked up some enthusiasm.

"Ella, that… was… AWESOME!!!"

She had rolled over on her back by this point and pulled her goggles off. She looked up at me and her slightly panicked look turned to one of sheer excitement.

"Yeah!" she said, her voice a unique mixture of excitement and the sound of a girl who just had the wind knocked out of her.

"You were flying! Ella, that was some run. You were so fast!"

She nodded and started to sit up. I helped her brush some of the snow off.

"Daddy, that was so cool!" I just smiled at her. She continued, "Was the crash awesome? Did you video it?"

I laughed and nodded slightly. Her face absolutely lit up. "Can I see?"

I helped her get her skis back on and she gave me a two thumbs up.

"Daddy, can we do it again?"

I nodded, smiled, closed my eyes and took a deep breath. "You bet we can!"

Snow and You

If you're not falling, every now and then – if you're not failing, every now and then – you're probably not at your potential. Maybe not even close. Are you chasing safety? Or are you chasing the impact you are capable of making? Do you fail often enough? When was the last time you went down a hill that you'd never gone down before? … you tried to stretch your business, your career, your parenting, one of your relationships – further than you'd gone before? When was the last time you went face first into the snow?

Sydney at Sunrise

Flying from New York City to Sydney, Australia is not something I would recommend doing on a regular basis. Sydney is a gorgeous city and New York is – well, New York – but the first time I made the trip, we left New York at 7 p.m. on a Friday evening. The sun was setting, and my plane would follow the sun's path around the earth for roughly 24 hours, allowing for a brief refueling stop in Los Angeles. My fellow passengers and I did not see the sun again until about a half an hour before landing in Sydney on Sunday morning. Full of excitement to see Sydney, I dragged my belongings from the airport to downtown, just in time to attend a church service in the architectural marvel that is St. Mary's Cathedral, adjacent to Hyde Park. That Sunday turned out to be an unbelievably beautiful sunny day, with the bluest sky and temperatures in the eighties... but I would not get to enjoy this day in its entirety.

My trip to Australia had been brought on through the request of a global entrepreneurship organization. I was there to speak to their members about Creative Leadership with a focus on becoming more creative as an individual and building a culture in your business that supports and sustains innovation. Since I had never made this trip and would be speaking on several consecutive days, I decided to allow an extra few days for some sightseeing and the chance to get used to the time change.

On that Sunday morning, I spent a few hours in downtown Sydney, caught my first glimpses of the Opera House, took a few dozen pictures of the landmark, and bought an unlimited subway, bus, and ferry pass for the week. Realizing that a lack of rest on the long flight and the disruption of a dramatic time difference was catching up with me, I took the train to my hotel and was checked in by early afternoon. I put my bags down in my room and thought a very brief nap might be refreshing. Refreshing it was. Brief it was not! When I bolted out of the bed, all was dark. Even though I didn't have anything set on the schedule for Monday, I was in a slight panic. What time was it? Why was it dark? I felt like I had slept very well and very long, but how could it still be dark? Then I remembered that I fell asleep in the early afternoon, perhaps around 1:30pm. I paced around the room, looking out my window and opening the door to the quiet hallway. What time was it? 12:17. It must have been 12:17 *AM*. The clock in my room read loud and clear. I called the front desk to check the time, thinking that the clock could be wrong, but it was not. I tried to get back to sleep. No luck. I grabbed a book and started to read, hoping this might help me get back to sleep. Unsuccessful. For about half an hour, I went back to reading, then I took out my laptop and took a look through some notes for my speeches that week. Slowly, I started to think about the questions I was pursuing, which progressed through a series, including:

- How can I get back to sleep?
- How can I quiet my mind?
- What can I do to be productive since I'm wide awake?
- What would be a better use of this time?

Then, I stopped everything, stood up and briskly walked around the room a few times before I stopped and stared into my own eyes reflected in the full-length mirror on one of the walls. Better questions. These questions were fine, but there were much better questions to ask. What would be a great question for this moment? I nodded at my reflection in the mirror. Yes! This little extra chunk of time was a gift. What could I do with this time that would create a memory that I would cherish for the rest of my life? That was a much better question than the first few I had been asking. Several answers started popping into my head and the one I would choose left me invigorated. I would get back to Circular Quay to see the Opera House at sunrise. Not only that, but I would ride the subway there and cross the famous Sydney Harbour Bridge. As the train crosses that bridge, you have an incredible view of the harbor and Opera House. I looked online for the subway schedule and found that the earliest of the day from my stop was 4:17am. I would be on the first train of the new day. I would be among the first passengers to commute into Sydney on that Monday morning. I still had some time before I would leave the hotel, so I kept my focus on the question of creating a memory to cherish throughout my lifetime. I decided to video the experience and you can see a clip with the rest of the book videos.

That morning, I had the chance to see the sun's first rays hit and reflect off the Sydney Opera House. There is very appropriate quote from Louis Kahn inside the Opera House: *"The sun did not know how beautiful its light was, until it was reflected off this building."*

When the design competition for the building was being planned, the group essentially asked, "How can we design a building for the arts that is suitable for the arts?" Many cities around the world have since borrowed inspiration from Sydney, asking, "What could be our version of the Sydney Opera House?" Seattle's Space Needle and San Antonio's Riverwalk are just two examples.

Before leaving my hotel for the subway station, I spent a few minutes online looking up Sydney destinations that might help with the creation of a lifelong memory. I already had a few places that I planned to visit, but as I searched online, I stumbled upon "I'm Free Tours." What? Although I rarely participate in formal tours, the title and the fact that I was looking to create a lifelong memory fed the intrigue. They run three free tours every single day. If you'd like to join one, all you need to do is show up at the tour's starting location at the designated time. No sign ups or payments are required. A guide in a green shirt that declares "I'M FREE" will greet you and off you go. Sustainability of the free tours comes from tips at the conclusion of each tour. Their website proudly proclaims:

Independently owned and unfunded.

We do not accept kickbacks or incentives and are completely unfunded by any government or private body. Wishing to remain unbiased and independent, we strive to inform all participates of the BEST LOCAL sights, stories, transport, activities, restaurants and bars to help them get to know our cities like we do.

You can learn more about them here: www.imfree.com.au I decided that I would join the tour at the start. It was scheduled to last about 2 ½ hours, and I could duck out if it wasn't what I hoped. Instead, it was more than I hoped. My guide that morning was Justine, the co-founder of I'm Free Tours in Sydney and Melbourne. She didn't mention this to the group, but I had decided to stay close to her to get the most out of the tour and, as we walked from place to place, I asked her about the tour and how she got involved. She proceeded to tell me about the early days of the business, which occurred only about five years prior. Since "what can I learn?" is question that I like to let affect each day of my life, I asked Justine many questions. She was a graduate student studying architecture when she and her fiancé, Ross, began the business. They were looking for jobs, and not finding something that fit the way they hoped. While they continued their job search, they decided to run a few tours. The couple had spent some time touring Europe and they both had a great appreciation for their own home city, so "I'm Free Tours" was launched. Justine let me know that they now had a full schedule every day in Sydney and Melbourne, as well as a growing staff with the same enthusiasm and knowledge about these cities. My tour group was about forty people, which was fairly typical, but not even close to the largest groups they would frequently draw. In addition to learning about the unique small business, the tour itself was also excellent. We saw film locations from the Matrix, a hospital funded by the sale of rum, and heard countless great stories, including a crowd favorite about two creative, artistic, and entrepreneurial protestors. Some in the crowd liked the story. Some hated it. Some both liked and hated the story.

In the wee morning hours of March 18, 2003, Will and Dave got to work. Hauling a collection of equipment for their project, they climbed to the top of the tallest sail of the magnificent series of buildings in Circular Quay, known worldwide as the Sydney Opera House. Once at the top, the two painted a graffiti message to the world in three coats of red paint:

NO WAR

The very next day, a coalition of nations would declare war on Iraq. The pair of men were punished for their vandalism, including a $151,000 fine to help pay for the clean up the Opera House sail. Most of the fine money was raised creatively. Will Saunders and Dave Burgess created and sold "No War Snow Globes" with a replica of the Opera House containing their red graffiti inside. Thousands of the snow globes were sold at $20 each.

Danish architect and designer of the Sydney Opera House, Jorn Utzon, even sent Will and Dave autographed photographs of the Opera House. When Utzon won the design competition in January of 1957, he could not have anticipated the challenges the project would bring. One of the judges arrived late to the design review and pulled Utzon's design, entry number 218, from the discarded pile. Although Utzon won the competition, he would never see the finished building with his own eyes. His design was selected, he would see pictures and videos of it, but Sydney did not allow him to return. While he oversaw construction, progress was extremely slow, and the budget was obliterated. To say that local officials were not pleased would be a dramatic understatement. But Sydney did eventually complete Utzon's Opera House. How many times have you heard, "Sydney Opera House – it's definitely on my bucket list. Right alongside the Eiffel Tower, Jerusalem, the Grand Canyon, and the Great Pyramids!

The last stop on our I'm Free Tour that Monday morning was one of the best places to photograph the Opera House. Virtually every tour attendee was still with us and most contributed with a meaningful tip. I did some math with rough estimates and have to say that Ross and Justine have found a great way to turn their passion and talent into a meaningful and profitable small business.

What could you do this year – this morning, or this weekend – that would create a memory you will cherish for the rest of your life?

Sam Never Arrived

"It all changed – *everything* – since Sam's been gone." The woman who told me this was a third shift supervisor at a distribution center on the East Coast. As she said the words, her eyes had a far-away look and I could see that she missed him; she missed *those* times. Her look said more, though. It said that something was so right about that time and something was so very wrong about this time. Something was so right about Sam's approach and something was equally wrong about the approach of his replacement. Replacement might be the wrong word here. Her whole demeanor made it clear that Sam could not have a replacement.

I wasn't sure she would answer with any details, but decided to ask, "What's different?" I expected another "Everything!" and that's exactly what she gave me. But then she continued.

"Everything…" There was a long pause as she warmed up and reflected. "He was like a regular guy. He didn't have any airs of self-importance. He'd come here in that old pickup truck and park out back just like everybody else. He'd walk around the warehouse, check things out, talk to people – just like you and I are doing here – normal conversation. He'd get to know you. He wasn't here that often, but when he'd come back, he'd remember us. If you told him you had kids or liked to fish, he'd remember that when he came back. He…" She stopped again and, even though Sam had passed away more than a decade ago, her emotions were palpable.

I wasn't sure if she would be able to continue, but was glad that she did. "Sure, he was busy! But he still talked to people like they were people. He'd ask how you liked the place, if there was anything you thought should be changed, what could make the work easier, help with costs or quality or safety. And he would listen. He seemed to listen like nobody else."

I was thankful for what she had shared, but her nugget of gold was still to come. Suddenly, she had this excited look on her face and her voice became louder and more animated.

"What's different? I'll tell you what's different!" I thought she already had, but this was it, this was the difference. "When he came to visit, he came into the real world, into our world. He might pop in the back door and help offload a truck. While he was doing that, side by side with us, Sam listened to everyone's ideas. Now, when we get a corporate visit, they go in the boardroom and look at PowerPoint slides. We don't even see them in the warehouse."

Decades before this conversation, Sam took his first job out of college as a management trainee with JC Penney in Des Moines, Iowa. One of Penney's corporate reps told Sam, "I'd fire you if you weren't such a good salesman. Maybe you're just not cut out for retail." Sam was not very good at the sales slips and cash register side of things. But even in his early twenties, Sam would go visit competitors during his lunch break. He walked over to the nearby Sears or Yonkers store to – in his own words – "see what they were up to."

When World War II interrupted every aspect of life, Sam still found ways to borrow lessons from others. While stationed with the Army in Salt Lake City, Utah, he checked out every single library book on retailing and visited local department stores to study their operations. Sam was an idea sponge.

In 1945, with just eighteen months of retail experience, Sam took a small loan from a family member and bought an existing Ben Franklin variety store franchise in Newport, Arkansas. It was a failing store, one of the worst in the whole company, and the owner wanted out. The business was overpriced, rent was exorbitant for the space, and the lease did not provide Sam with an option to renew, but he dove in head-first. How many of us have been thinking about some great idea for years, even decades, without taking action? Describing that early experience, Sam said, "You can learn from everybody. I probably learned the most from studying what John Dunham was doing across the street." Initially, that store across the street had more than double the revenue of Sam's store.

Sam said, "At the very beginning, I went along and ran my store by their book [the Ben Franklin franchise system] because I really didn't know any better. But it didn't take me long to start experimenting..." Experimentation would take him into all different areas, including extensive experimentation on pricing, purchasing, how to get people into the store, how to find, filter, and attract the best people, who to buy from, product offerings, store size and location. Sam doubled his store's volume in the first two years and had completely paid back his initial loan by the third year, but said, "As good as business was, I never could leave well enough alone, and, in fact, I think my constant fiddling and meddling with the status quo may have been one of my biggest contributions to the later success..." When the initial five-year lease expired, Sam had the store delivering three and a half times initial revenues, and the property owner decided not to let Sam renew the lease. Instead, the landlord gave what was now a very profitable store location to his own son. Over those five years, Sam's experiments and enthusiasm had taken the store from losing money to making a profit of about $40,000 a year in 1950. Adjusted for inflation, that's close to $450,000 in 2023 dollars. But now, Sam was a retailer without a store.

Instead of giving up, Sam found a new location in a different town and this time, he signed a 99-year lease. Referencing Sam's approach to learning and failure, biographer John Huey said, "I don't think there's any way that he could have failed, ultimately."

Over the next few years, Sam opened several additional Ben Franklin franchises, but continued to experiment in just about every area possible. When Sam saw self-serve retail in the 1950s, he immediately decided to be one of the first retailers to give it a shot. He even approached Ben Franklin's management and proposed to be their guinea pig with franchised discount stores in rural communities. Their model was variety stores, not discounting, and they turned him down. By now, you probably realize that this rejection didn't stop Sam. He opened a discount store outside of the Ben Franklin franchise with his own name on it, the "Walton Five and Dime."

Then, in 1962, seventeen years after buying his first retail franchise, Sam Walton founded Wal-Mart, and two decades later, Sam's Club.

In his autobiography, Sam tried to boil his success down to 10 rules, writing, "They are some rules that worked for me. But I always prided myself on breaking everybody else's rules and I always favored the mavericks who challenged my rules.... So pay special attention to rule 10... It could mean simply: Break All the Rules." Of Sam's 10 rules, here are two of my personal favorites:

RULE 7: Listen to everyone in your company. And figure out ways to get them talking.... to force good ideas to bubble up within it [the organization], you must listen to what your associates are trying to tell you.

RULE 10: "Swim Upstream. Go the other way. Ignore the conventional wisdom. If everybody else is doing it one way, there's a good chance you can find your niche by going in exactly the opposite direction. But be prepared for a lot of folks to wave you down and tell you you're headed the wrong way. I guess in all my years, what I heard more often than anything was: a town of less than 50,000 population cannot support a discount store for very long.

From what I understand about Sam Walton's personality, if he were to meet you, he would expect to learn a lot from you. Let's flip the tables today and learn from him!

A Master at Collecting Ideas

"Sam would take his executives around to the worst store that he could come up with, and he would say, 'This is a horrible store. I want everybody to come out of there with one thing they do better than we do because everybody does something good. And there's something in there that we could do.'" - *John Huey, Biographer*

In the 1980s, a group of Brazilian businessmen wrote letters to a dozen U.S. retail leaders, including Sam Walton, hoping to set up a visit to learn about their retail operations. Most of the U.S. retailers didn't respond. A few politely declined. Sam Walton, on the other hand, invited the group to Bentonville, Arkansas, personally picked them up at the airport, and proceeded to ask his visitors question after question about business in South America. When the group returned the favor and invited Sam to Brazil, one of the businessmen received a late afternoon phone call from the police in Sao Paolo. Sam had been arrested for conducting some of his retail studies while crawling around in stores on his hands and knees to measure aisle widths!

Don Soderquist, who would later become Wal-Mart's CEO, was in charge of data processing at Ben Franklin when he met Sam in 1964. During that first meeting, Sam asked Soderquist all kinds of questions about possible computer usage in retail. The very next day, Soderquist was shopping in at a K-Mart near his house when he noticed Sam Walton talking to one of the clerks. Soderquist said:

"I just rolled up behind him and I could hear him asking the clerk, 'How frequently do you order?... How much do you order?... And if you order on a Tuesday, when does the merchandise come in?' He's writing everything she says down a little blue spiral notebook. Then Sam gets down on his hands and knees and he's looking under this stack table, and he opens the sliding doors and says, 'How do you know

how much you've got under here when you're placing that order?' Finally, I said, 'Sam Walton, is that you?'"

When Soderquist asked him what he was doing, Sam simply said "Oh, this is just part of the educational process. That's all." Sam never stopped this educational process, although he did eventually replace his notebooks with a little tape recorder.

Retail Consultant, Kurt Barnard, described a similar experience in his first meeting with Sam in 1967: "...he proceeded to extract every piece of information in your possession. He always makes little notes.... I wasn't sure what I had just met, but I was sure we would hear more from him." That first conversation was supposed to last ten minutes, but Sam asked questions for two and a half hours."

On family vacations, Sam's children recall their father stopping to visit stores on practically every journey. The stores he visited weren't Wal-Marts, they were stores of just about any type imaginable. Whether they were camping in the Adirondacks or Ozarks, Sam would map out stores to visit for miles around their camp sites. Many people will say that you can learn from everyone. Sam Walton actually lived this philosophy and expected it from his entire organization. Permit a powerful side note: if we don't love the work we are involved in, is this level of consistent study likely – or even possible?

On one family vacation to England, a shop sign in London caught Sam's attention. He pointed the sign out to his wife, Helen, and said, "Look at that sign. That's what we should do." The company's sign listed all their associates. Wal-Mart would now describe employees as associates and implemented profit-sharing for all associates starting in 1972. In addition to stock ownership, over 75% of Wal-Mart store management started out as hourly associates.

When Sam and Helen visited a tennis ball manufacturer in Japan, Sam noticed that they began the day with calisthenics as a group.

He absolutely loved the idea and couldn't wait to get home to try it out in the stores.

Sam was once eating lunch with a reporter in a small-town restaurant near his home. At one point, Sam pointed out another diner and noted that the man owned a small business in the area. Sam went on to mention that he planned to have a conversation with the small business owner and said, "I can learn a lot from him." Sam's net worth at the time was already in the billions. *I can learn a lot from him!* How often do we take that approach? Sam's brother Bud recalls, "There may not be anything (Sam) enjoys more than going into a competitor's store trying to learn something."

How did he build idea collection into the company's culture? One secret lies in his perspective: "There is only one boss. The customer. And he can fire everybody in the company from the chairman on down, simply by spending his money somewhere else."

It was not unusual for an associate to drive to Bentonville – often hundreds of miles and many hours from their home – to speak with Sam. In the early 1990s, David Glass asked, "How many chairmen of $50 billion companies do you know who are totally, 100% accessible to their hourly associates?" In Sam's own words: "I get tremendously excited... talking with our associates and drinking coffee with them... It's amazing to me how many ideas they always have for fine-tuning the system." When accepting the presidential medal of freedom, Sam said, "The greatest thing is that we've got ideas from all 380,000 people in the company [Walmart's associate count is over 2.3 million as I write this]. That's the best part." Many in leadership roles say things like this, but as Sam said these words, you could see, hear, and feel his sincerity.

If you knew that your boss, teacher, spouse, peers, or friends were that interested in hearing your ideas, and perhaps even implementing many of them, how many more ideas and perspectives would you share? Flip it around. How often have you not shared ideas because you were convinced that the people around you were not interested?

Experimenting

David Glass, who would later become CEO of Wal-Mart and is currently the owner of the Kansas City Royals, first encountered Sam Walton in 1964 at the grand opening of the second Wal-Mart.

"When I saw the Harrison [Arkansas] store, I thought to myself, this is absolutely the worst discount store or retail store that I've ever seen. Sam bought a couple of truckloads of watermelons and he'd stacked them up across the front of the store. He had donkey rides for the kids out on the parking lot... and what he didn't anticipate is that the temperature was about 110° in Harrison that day. The watermelons began to pop and that watermelon juice began to run all over the parking lot and the donkeys did what donkeys do and sort of tracked through all that. You can imagine what it looked like. It all mixed together and ran all over the parking lot. And when you went inside the store, the mess just continued, having been tracked in all over the floor. He was a nice fellow, but I wrote him off. It was just terrible. The thing I didn't realize about Sam though, and the people who were involved in those early days in Walmart, is that they had a quality that I haven't seen in many people or in many companies... Never a day went by that they didn't improve something."

Glass was far from impressed but liked Walton enough to tell him the truth... that he thought it was the worst store he'd ever seen and that he ought to try something different. Decades later, Glass said, "Two things about Sam Walton distinguish him from almost everyone else I know. First, he gets up every day determined to improve something. Second, he is less afraid of being wrong than anyone I've ever known. And once he sees he's wrong, he just shakes it off and heads in another direction."

Those two traits led to rapid growth and a unique set of challenges; one of the biggest was finding and retaining great people. Sam wasn't willing to compromise on bringing in the best people possible, so despite extremely limited cashflow especially in the early days, Walton often promised new managers a percentage of their store's profits. Many early managers were even asked to invest their own money in the launch of their stores. This expression of Sam's might be his way of describing the Innovator's Equation. "Capital isn't scarce; vision is."

Often after store visits, Sam would recommend that someone he'd interacted with that day be given a store to manage. In response to questions about the person's experience, Sam was fond of saying, "Give him a store anyway. Let's see how he does." *Less afraid of being wrong than anyone I've ever known!*

THE WORST WAL-MART

Walmart store number 880 in Irving, Texas had the worst shrinkage of any Walmart. Shrinkage measures merchandise that is lost, usually via theft, and Irving's was about 6%. In a company that averages just over 3% net profit, consistently losing 6% of inventory would be fatal. Sam talked to the district manager, Ed Nagy. Within a year-and-a-half, shrinkage was down from 6% to 2%. Sam later described Nagy: "…he likes to try new things, and, I have to admit, he reminds me a bit of myself as a youngster." Part of Nagy's approach included getting managers from that store to rub shoulders with folks from the successful stores in his district. This changed the managers' belief, their expectation, of what they thought was possible. Then Nagy let them set their own goals.

Andy Sims, the manager Walmart #1 in Rogers, Arkansas, said, "[Sam] is a master at erasing that 'larger-than-life' feeling that people have for him. How many heads of state always start the conversation by wanting to know what you think? What's on your mind? After a visit, everyone in the store has no doubt that he genuinely appreciates our contributions, no matter how insignificant. Every associate feels like he or she does make a difference. It's almost like having your oldest friend come just to see if you're okay. He never lets us down."

On early New York City buying trips, Sam would try to instill in the team that we don't do things the way everyone else does them. Describing those buying trips, store manager Gary Reinboth said, "We always walked everywhere, never took cabs." Sam's equation for the trips: expenses should never exceed 1% of all purchases. They shared crowded little hotel rooms. While New York City businesses wanted everyone to meet during their normal business hours, Sam would get someone to meet with them outside of normal hours on both sides of the day. He kept his team extremely busy for the entire trip, getting people to change their rules. Reinboth said, "I think he was trying to make a point: just because we're in New York doesn't mean we have to start doing things their way." Do you challenge others' perceived limitations to catalyze creativity?

This letter to the Wal-Mart team shares a glimpse of Sam:

6/1/1982 "Is there a better way? How can we further reduce our prices and our expenses? What should our stores look like five years out? Together we have to keep searching and finding those better ways. I've long been a student and admirer of K-mart, and my present opinion is that they're doing a great many things right and will progressively improve their program and remain a very viable and good tough competitor for us for years to come.... [Sam went on to speak about several other competitors and lessons that could be borrowed.] So it goes, my friends. Competition. We've always had it and always will. It will get better and stronger, but you know what we've always said. Competition is the essence of Free Enterprise. Competition is great. Let them come on. It just makes us better. And you and I know that it has and does work that way for Wal-Mart. We will compete and we will continue to listen to our customers and to each other. That's our Wal-Mart way. We care – and we, too, will keep improving and someday become one of the truly great retail companies of the world. I've rambled, my friends..."

GETTING PEOPLE TO VISIT THE STORES

Sam was a master at trying out ideas, saying, "We tried literally to create a carnival atmosphere in our stores." Experiments included sidewalk sales, bands, circuses, sailing paper plates from store rooftops with a product name and special price, balloon drops with discounts, Moonlight Madness sales with a new bargain or promotion being announced every few minutes, shopping cart bingo where every shopping cart had a number on it and if your number was called you to get a percentage discount on every single thing that you currently had in the cart, free boxes of candy to people who had traveled the farthest to get to the store. Sam said, "As long as it was fun, we'd try it. Occasionally it would blow up in our face." One store in Fayetteville celebrated Washington's birthday on February 22nd by selling a television set for $0.22. The hitch was you had to find that TV. It was hidden somewhere in the store and the first person to find it could purchase if for just $0.22. On that day, the store was completely overwhelmed with shoppers and the store manager decided to discontinue merchandise "hide-and-seek". A Nebraska store formed a *Precision Shopping Cart Drill Team* that marched – and performed – in local parades. A store in Georgia held a *Kiss a Pig* contest. They set up donation jars for local charities and labeled each jar with a manager's name. At the end of the fund raiser, the manager whose jar had the most donations got to kiss a pig. In Louisiana, associates formed a cheerleading squad called the *Shrink Cats* who cheered mostly about shrinkage. Sam's early days with Wal-Mart stores exemplified "build-build-build-build-jump". Store contests included poetry, singing, and the most beautiful baby. Theme days would find associates dressed up in costumes. An Oklahoma store buried $36 in coins in a pile of hay and let kids dive in to find money. Fashion shows used store associates as models. An assistant manager in Alabama accidentally ordered four times too many Moon Pies – a chocolate, graham cracker, and marshmallow treat – but he promptly came up with the idea of a Moon Pie eating contest, which soon become an annual October tradition in that store.

The teams essentially asked, "What could be a lot of fun and get people to come to our stores?" and "How can we create an atmosphere where experimenting, putting ideas out there, and trying things is more than okay, it's actually expected?"

Sam lived his phrase, "To succeed in this world, you have to change all the time." Occasionally, he would interrupt meetings, point at someone and say, "Okay, you run the meeting today."

At most of the corporate Saturday morning meetings, the team would dig into one single store, looking at every aspect of that store. Often, they would not only come up with great strategies or solutions for that store's current challenges, but they would also learn a few lessons from that store that could be applied in other locations. David Glass said, "No other company does that.... What we guard against around here is people saying, 'Let's think about it.' We make a decision then we act on it. If we make a decision on Friday, we expect it to be acted on in all the stores on Saturday." Claude Harris, store manager and the first buyer for Walmart, recalls a common phrase of Sam's: "Go ahead and try it."

Sam's own children had paper routes. He felt that kind of thing was critical for training them about success. Sam's son, John, recalls being twelve years old and asking his father for permission to climb a bluff overlooking the Buffalo River. Sam said, "Do anything you're big enough to do."

A Few Interesting Programs

Eat What You Cook: This was one of Sam's favorite programs. Every quarter, each buyer spends a few days in a store as acting manager in the department for which she buys merchandise. What a great reality check for the buyers!

VPI (Volume Producing Item): Everyone, from department managers up, can select one item to promote in just about any way they choose. Whoever creates the most sales on their item wins. One winner loaded a dirty pickup truck with car wash items and parked the truck inside the store.

Greeters: In 1980, Sam met the first Wal-Mart greeter in a Louisiana store. The store manager, Dan McAllister, had a shrinkage problem, so the greeter served two functions: a friendly welcoming face and a warning to someone who might want to steal.

Philanthropy: "We are going to approach philanthropy with the same lack of reverence we gave to the traditional methods of the retail business when we started out there. We are going to see if we can shake up some of the time-honored assumptions..." In just one area of philanthropy, Sam said, "Frankly, I'd like to see an all-out revolution in education." Proceeds from his autobiography went to an organization focused on *break-the-mold* education.

What would Sam do today?

Don Soderquist, former Wal-mart CEO said, "His vision was to reduce the cost of living for the people who shop in our stores.... the second part of his vision was do it with a group of people who believe in what he believed in.... more than anything, I watched how he treated people... Sam genuinely cared about other people...

Sam would talk to people... who were unloading a trailer in the middle of summer, sweaty... he treated them no different than he treated the president of the United States... because in Sam's mind, we're all equal... Sam viewed his role in the company of being the person who showed and demonstrated respect for everybody... you can watch how people treat waiters and waitresses and you can tell a little bit about them... he was a very, very humble man."

Just before he passed away in 1992, Sam discussed his belief that Wal-Mart would reach $100 Billion in total revenue by the year 2000. In Sam's words, "Nothing like it has ever been done before, but our folks will do it. And now I'm going to confess a really radical thought I've been having lately. I probably won't do anything about it, but the folks who come after me are eventually going to have to face up to this question.... can a $100 billion retailer really function as efficiently and productively as it should? Or would maybe five $20 billion companies work better?" They finished 1992 with $56 Billion in sales, passed the $100 Billion mark in 1996, and $200 Billion in 2001.

What would Sam do today? Three things are certain: Sam would learn something. Sam would change something. And Sam would genuinely care about the people he encountered today!

Isaac Newton Visits the Fair

"If I have seen further, it is by standing upon the shoulders of giants." ~ *Isaac Newton*

We have all had a similar experience. Something caught your attention, aroused your curiosity. What steps do you take next?

Cambridge in the summer was a bustling town. The famous Sturbridge Fair was begun in 1199 by King John, signer of the Magna Carta and villainized in Robin Hood folklore. At the Sturbridge Fair, just 466 years later on a Sunday afternoon in the summer of 1665, Isaac Newton would make two small but notable purchases: Euclid's *Elements* and a simple glass prism. His curiosity piqued, Newton rushed back to his room with his new purchases and began to experiment. With the curtains drawn, he fed this curiosity and allowed a beam of sunlight to pass through the prism. He changed the conditions, including the angle, amount of light, and which surface of the prism the light would strike first. Then Newton cut a small hole in a piece of cardboard to control the light more precisely. Since the prism had long been considered nothing more than a child's toy, so-called *normal* scientists had never bothered to conduct significant experiments with them.

When a beam of sunlight passed through the single prism, that colorless light, known as white light, burst into a spectrum of color. Newton wondered if the prism contained the color, created the color, or if the original beam of sunlight contained this full spectrum. Before long, Newton's curiosity and imagination led him back to ye old Sturbridge Fair, where he purchased another prism to expand the experiment.

Upon returning to his room, Newton used the second prism to translate the spectrum back into white light. Interesting! But Isaac Newton was not one to settle or to curb his curiosity. Next, he cut a slit in a piece of paper and placed that paper between the two prisms.

He aligned the slit to block all the colors of the spectrum except red. What would happen when only red light went through the second prism? The red beam of light remained red. The direction of the light was changed, but the red light did not turn back into white light.

Through this simple experiment, Newton had discovered that sunlight contains all the shades of the spectrum. The prism, previously considered a mere child's toy, had helped to uncover one of the greatest mysteries behind our interaction with the visible world.

Did he let this finding satisfy his curiosity and imagination? Was this enough experimentation?

For Newton, it was not. Newton would go on to discover some of the most important laws for describing the behavior of our universe. Not only that, but to do so, he developed a new type of mathematics, *The Calculus*. High school students around the globe likely utter this one word, Calculus, with more emotion than any other course or subject.

The gap between being overwhelmed in Calculus class and inventing Calculus: massive. The gap between not questioning and questioning: massive. The gap between mediocre questions, good questions and great questions: massive. The gap between asking a great question once in a while and pursuing a great question: massive. The gap between being curious when the mood strikes you and intentionally feeding your curiosity, letting it carry you away: massive.

In his own words, Newton described his willingness to feed his curiosity: "I do not know what I may appear to the world, but to myself I seem to have been only like a boy playing on the sea-shore, and diverting myself in now and then finding a smoother pebble or a prettier shell than ordinary, whilst the great ocean of truth lay all undiscovered before me."

Many of us hesitate to experiment for fear we might look silly, to avoid hurting our pride. Some of Newton's experimenting went beyond emotional pain and, in fact, presented possible physical danger. For example, as a boy, Newton would look at the sun – something his sensible mother had told him never to do. He even experimented with staring at the reflection of the sun in a mirror until he temporarily lost his sight. Afterwards, he shut himself up in a dark room for several *days*, until his vision finally returned. As a parent with two children who will find themselves studying Calculus in a few years, I think I'll refrain from sharing this anecdote with my children until they've completed at least a year of Calculus. After that, we can discuss whether or not this mathematics was invented by a creative genius, a verifiable lunatic, or both!

Imagine that you are a college student. As you walk across the campus with a few friends, you see a professor on the roof of a three-story building. As you approach, you realize that he's dropping things off the roof. You and your friends have a good laugh, but as you get closer to the building, a friend asks, "Isn't that your professor for that 3 o'clock class?" You nod, and your friend continues, "*That*... must be one interesting class!" While Newton worked on understanding gravity, he could often be seen dropping things from the roof of the three-story building at Cambridge where he lived. As a professor, his courses were rarely well-attended and, quite frequently, no one showed up at all. Imagine looking back and recalling that you skipped Isaac Newton's classes regularly!

Reflective Telescope

Newton lived in an age of lackluster telescopes. Even the best models of the day used glass lenses for magnification and Newton's experiments with prisms verified that lenses refracted different colors at different angles. The result: a magnified, but fuzzy, image for the viewer. To create a clearer image, Newton experimented with curved mirrors instead of lenses. A large mirror would capture

159

the image, then a smaller mirror would bounce it into the viewer's eye. Newton's method produced a much clearer image and allowed for a much shorter telescope. Although a Scottish mathematician had proposed this idea earlier, Newton was the first to build a working model of the reflective telescope, even grinding the mirrors himself. Newton's prototype was just 6 inches long with a magnifying power of 40x and was presented to the Royal Society in 1670.

Coins

You've undoubtedly held a U.S. quarter in your hand. The coin has ridges along the outer rim. Newton invented this concept as a solution to coin shaving, a practice of cutting small amounts of valuable metal off the outer edges of coins. Shaved coins also made counterfeiting much easier and more commonplace in Newton's time. The treasury department asked Newton to help solve this problem. Which creative minds should you get involved in solving some of your current challenges? Perhaps they're not even in your industry!

Law of Cooling

Newton pursued questions about the cooling of a hot iron. His default approach seemed to be, "I wonder…" followed by experimentation. Experiments with cooling hot objects showed that temperature change is proportional to the difference in temperature between the object and its surroundings: Newton's Law of Cooling.

Notebook

Newton sectioned his notebook and constantly collected ideas and questions pertaining to each of these 45 sections. His curiosity covered many themes, including light, color, gravity, planets, philosophy, matter, and spirituality. His voracious reading – including Descartes, Moore, and Euclid – was a catalyst for ideas and Newton was often so involved in his studies or an experiment that he forgot to eat.

Lost in the Wind

When he was a child, Isaac's mother sent him outside during a terrible wind storm to ensure that the buildings, doors, windows, and fences were sufficiently secured. Isaac went out but did not return quickly. He looked at the strong wind blowing things all around and began to wonder… After substantial waiting, his mother went outside to find young Isaac jumping off a fence repeatedly to see how far the wind would carry him. He alternated the direction of his jumps, jumping as far as he could with the wind and then against the wind, measuring the jump distances for comparison.

On the day that Oliver Cromwell died, September 3, 1658, there was a great storm throughout England. Newton repeated his jumping experiment and compared those leaps with those made during other storms and on calm days. After this storm, Newton puzzled other neighborhood boys by explaining that this had been a foot stronger than any he'd experienced. He alleviated their confusion by showing them the marks of his leaps from the series of experiments, his own storm measurement system.

Isaac often locked himself in the room at his grandmother's house and spent the whole day making models, kites, sundials, and other mechanical devices. One handy device was a folding lantern made of crumpled paper. He would light his way to school on dark winter mornings and fold the lantern up for storage in his classroom.

Along with a love of the wind came a love of kites. Newton even flew kites at night and a version of his light-weight crumpled paper lantern could be flown beneath a kite to create an eerie floating glow. Young Newton stopped flying the lantern at night when some neighbors thought it might start a fire while others carried suspicions that the floating light was a ghost or witch.

Wind or Mouse?

The construction of a windmill near Newton's home captured his insatiable curiosity. Mills powered by water were much more common in this region of 17th century England. Newton walked by the construction site after school each day to observe progress and analyze the design. He decided to build a miniature replica, using cloth for sails and mounting it on his roof. Reliance on wind for power frustrated Newton, so he built a "back-up generator" – a wheel powered by a mouse (nicknamed Mouse Miller) to keep the miniature windmill going. Unfortunately, this "back-up generator" often ate the corn that the mill was grinding.

Thought Experiments and the Moon

From the records of his work, I expect that Newton's conversations with himself often started with words like these:

Imagine this...

What if...

I wonder...

Feeding his fascination around the paths of moving bodies, Newton conducted many "thought experiments," including one that set the table for satellites to orbit the earth three hundred years later. Newton imagined a cannon mounted on a very high mountain. The mountain was so high that it reached through the earth's atmosphere to a point where there would be no air resistance to slow down the cannonball. Next, he imagined that the cannon could be fired with different amounts of gunpowder, launching the cannonball at various speeds. While in flight, gravity between the cannonball and earth would cause the cannonball to fall towards the earth. However, if the cannonball were fired at the correct speed ("orbital speed"), the cannonball would fall towards the earth at the same speed as the earth's spherical surface was "falling away" from the cannonball's initial linear path. The ball would then continue to orbit the earth without ever falling from the sky or launching into space. The ball would be in orbit around the earth, just like the moon.

How many great thought experiments can you create beginning with "Imagine this…" or "What if…" or "I wonder…"?

Actions to Expand Your Creativity

What would be more fitting that ending this chapter by applying Newton's 1st Law of motion to your creativity? An object at rest tends to stay at rest and an object in motion tends to stay in motion. Let's get your creativity in motion! Nurture your curiosity and imagination. You (and your organization) will remain as creative today as you were yesterday unless something is done to catalyze a change. Why not be the change?

Build a color wheel. Go on the roof or to a 2nd story window and drop different objects. Time the decent. Measure heavy wind by jumping or throwing objects with and against it. Project the moonlight (or a solar eclipse) through a pinhole. Build a small windmill. Make a bungie swing to hang from a tree. Disassemble a child's toy. Experiment with cooling liquids quickly. Make a sun dial. Build a catapult or slingshot. Make a small batch of homemade maple syrup, apple cider, mulled wine, or beer. Make two batches of the same beer but ferment it with two different yeasts to see the impact. Create your own version of a card game or a kick-ball tournament for 2 player teams. Get in motion!

Uber University

The world is full of interesting people! Interesting is only one of many descriptive phrases we could use here. I don't always use Uber, but when I do, I *try* to go into the experience expecting a great lesson or perspective. Is it easy to keep that mindset? Not usually, but when I am able to keep that expectancy, humbly ask a few questions, and patiently pay attention to the answers, the reward is a great lesson more often than not.

On July 13, 2016, Dallas was hot, humid, and uncomfortable. It was just a few days after five police officers were killed in an ambush. The tension was palpable. I landed in the Dallas Fort Worth International Airport just after 6pm and the temperature was a very sticky and uncomfortable 100°. The air felt like you could squeeze water from it and everyone waiting to be picked up at the curb was feeling the heat. After a few minutes, my Uber driver arrived and we headed downtown. My keynote the next morning was just blocks away from JFK's infamous grassy knoll and the recent police ambush.

The driver and I made small talk for a few minutes. He asked me the normal questions: "Have you been to Dallas before? How long are you staying? What brings you here?" Cliché questions that guide cliché conversations. Our culture loves cliché conversations. They go nowhere, thus avoiding the potential for both differing opinions and meaningful connection. As soon as we share our opinions, we're sharing a little bit of what we believe and why we believe it. Dangerous. What if we let people see who we really are, our true selves, and they don't like what they find? On the other hand, what if people like us for who we pretend to be? Is that a recipe for great relationships?

I asked my driver how long he had been driving with Uber and how he got into it. A "what got you started doing ____" question often facilitates connection. My driver, Josh, said that he had started his own business – a skateboard brand – and wanted something with the flexibility to support his business launch. Apparently, my driver had been a professional skateboarder for many years. Here is a brief excerpt from our conversation:

Me: "That's intriguing. Professional skateboarding! Was it here in Dallas?"

Josh: "Yeah, and I got to travel all over."

Me: "Sounds like a lot of fun. Was it?"

Josh: "You know it. Sometimes a little too much fun."

Me: "What do you mean, too much fun?"

Josh: "I partied too much. Way too much."

He went on to explain that he wanted to build a different kind of skateboard brand, a brand that stood for something. Not a brand that sold out. Life had taken him on a trip. His brand and skateboard designs would speak to the heart and soul of skateboarders like him. He had met so many along his journey. He wanted his story, his experiences, his difficulties to help his fellow boarders.

I could see and hear the emotion at this point. I paused briefly, and then said, "Life gives us some stuff, doesn't it? What kind of stuff did you have to go through?" Would he be willing to take the conversation deeper? He paused and collected himself before explaining that it was February 21st of 2011. He was holding his 18-month-old son, Flip (perfect name for the son of a professional skate-boarder!), when he decided that he would be a different father than his father had been. That night, cold turkey, Josh quit drinking a massive quantity of beer nightly and stopped using a wide assortment of drugs. Josh told me that his own father is in prison in Oklahoma and the two have never met. Josh said, "I decided that I could either be like him or take that experience to fuel my choice to make a change in my life, to take a different path, to be a different father to my son than my father was for me. My father's path didn't have to be mine. He made his choices and I would make mine. I don't know why he made the choices that he did, but I could choose to be a different dad to my son. I could even choose to love the dad that I had never met. I had that ability and I would exercise it. On February 21st, I chose a different path."

Josh became be very quiet and we let the seconds pass as we approached our exit.

I quietly said, "What a journey. What a powerful decision."

With a big smile, he said, "Yeah. Hasn't been easy. But it's been worth it. My son is everything."

One of my wonderful mentors loves to say that the word decision comes from the Latin word, *decidere*, which means "to cut off from." To cut off from any other path or option. Josh's decision certainly was that. He cut off his old way of life, including most of his friendships, as these old friends had not made the same decision to get rid of drinking, drugs, or bitterness towards some imperfect role model. After that decision, Josh cleaned himself up, got a job with a bank, added part time hours with Uber, saved money, then started a skateboard company on a bootstrap budget. He paid off the initial investment in less than 18 months. He chose the bootstrap route because he didn't want investors with agendas that might compromise the brand. He did not want the brand to sell out for revenue goals or investment priorities. You can find amazing skateboarding videos of Josh Hurley on YouTube and his brand at www.NowSkateboards.com.

I thanked Josh for sharing a bit of his incredible journey and mentioned that his son is very blessed. Then, I asked about some of the most powerful lessons he's learned. Josh told me that "Failure and the pavement are a skateboarder's classroom, teacher, best friend."

We still had a few minutes of traffic to deal with en route to my hotel, and I asked Josh about the atmosphere in Dallas. He said,

"You know, some people want to make this into a black and white thing, a race thing; but it's not that at all." He paused, and I looked at him in the rearview mirror, waiting for him to continue. He said, "It's not. It's about love and hate. A battle between love and hate." He pointed out the window and said, "The battle is not out there." He pointed to his own heart and said, "The battle is right here. You and I… every day and every moment we get to choose. As individuals, we get to decide. In this moment, will I choose love or choose hate?"

Each person we meet has experiences that we don't, has dealt with issues that we have not. For example, being a parent is an experience that you can try to explain from many, many different angles, but unless the person you're talking with has children of their own, they won't likely grasp the radical impact it has on every facet of life.

Josh's choice to be a different father than what he had experienced helped him to see the situation in Dallas differently than most people. His story inspired me to take a 3 mile walk through downtown Dallas that evening. When I left my hotel, it was still light out, but it was dark by the time I returned. The temperature was still in the 90s with very high humidity, but that didn't bother me anymore. I wanted to feel the love and the hate, the humidity and the heat, to feel the choices, to feel the tension, to try to help my heart to choose love. My walk took me through many different neighborhoods. I walked past many people. Was I nervous? Yes, absolutely. As I walked, I thought about Josh. I thought about Josh's father and I thought about Josh's son. Each time I passed by a person or group of people on those Dallas streets, I reminded myself to think about that person, knowing that each person had to deal with some "stuff." Every single person I passed had experiences that I would never have. They probably had some great role models. And they probably had some that were far from great. They had moments where they chose love and moments when they chose hate; and moments when they were somewhere between the two. That night, I let Dallas affect me. I let Josh affect me.

Josh was my Uber driver in a very hot and heated Dallas in the summer of 2016. I thank him from the bottom of heart for owning his choices and for sharing a part of his incredible journey and perspective.

Savannah, Georgia!

Adopting Families! One of the best sentences of advice I've ever received: Spend time with people who make you uncomfortable in a good way. My taxi ride in Savannah, Georgia, provided just that.

Pablo seemed friendly enough. I sat in the back seat and made small talk as we drove towards the Savannah Historic District. At one point, I asked if he drove full time. His answer, "Yes, but not really," begged a follow-up question. When I asked what he meant, the explanation left me in awe.

Pablo was currently working two full-time jobs. After I made a comment about doing what it takes to make ends meet, he humbly assured me that this was not the case. I hope the story that soft-spoken Pablo shared will make you as uncomfortable as it continues to make me. I had to pull most of the details out of him. Several years prior, Pablo and his wife were discussing generosity and purpose. They had taken a trip with a church group to Honduras, the country of Pablo's ancestry, and the deep needs of the Hondurans touched their hearts. As a lower middle-class family with four young children living in coastal Georgia, they didn't have much money left over at the end of each month. That trip to Honduras had taken some significant fund-raising efforts. Pablo's kids wore hand-me downs and never had the latest designer fashion clothing. The family of six lived in a small but comfortable 2-bedroom apartment, never ate in restaurants but never went to bed hungry. Under these circumstances, Pablo and his wife were discussing gratitude, generosity, how fortunate they were, and how they wanted to give back. He told me, "You do not have to be rich to be generous. Generosity is giving more than you can, more than is comfortable."

Pablo and his wife decided to adopt (via financial support) a child in Honduras. They researched organizations, found one that aligned with their plan, and set up a monthly contribution to sponsor one child. The monthly cost to sponsor that first child was less than half of what the average American family spends on their monthly cable/internet/Netflix bill. After a few months, Pablo and his wife sponsored another child, and then another and another. He seemed embarrassed as he shared this, but his passion for these kids was contagious. I could feel that passion in his voice. He told me the names and stories of several children. I told him that it sounded like he really knew the kids. He nodded and smiled. I assumed that he learned about them from a distance, but was overwhelmed when he enthusiastically exclaimed, "We visit them!" Pablo asked to work overtime for several months and the family decided to spend their vacation visiting their new "brothers and sisters". Instead of gifts under their Christmas tree, the family of six flew to Honduras. After that very first trip together, they were hooked! Their own children unanimously asked if they could visit again the following year, even if it meant making more sacrifices. One of their children included visiting Honduras in a letter to Santa that year. The family sponsored more children. In addition to an annual visit, Pablo's family writes, emails, and calls the children throughout the year. Eventually, Pablo started driving with Uber so that he could sponsor more children, and when I had the privilege of being his passenger, he was holding down a full-time job as well as driving full-time hours with Uber. Pablo's own children are older now, but they still make an annual family journey to Honduras to spend time with their extended family.

As we pulled up to the hotel for my conference, a quiet came over me. I realized that my bank and credit card statements are spiritual documents. They show who and what I worship. I could have stayed in a less expensive hotel and been generous with the savings.

I was silent as I thought about the impact Pablo was having half the world away. Working two jobs, not for a fancy car or TV, but for children most of us might not even realize exist. Somewhere along the ride, Pablo told me, "My wife and I, we decided to be generous with what little we had because we knew what it was like to have nothing."

Before he stopped the car, I asked Pablo how many children his family sponsors every month. His eyes met mine in the rearview mirror briefly before he looked down. He didn't want to tell me. A few seconds passed. "It's an amazing thing that you're doing. How many kids do you sponsor? Is it more than 10?" He nodded slightly. "15? 20?" He made a very subtle upward motion with his head. "More?" His head nodded upward again. "30?" Once again, his head tilted upward. I stopped breathing for a moment as the realization swept over me.

"Pablo, thank you. You are a gift."

He smiled softly, looked down, and whispered, "The children are a gift."

The car stopped. Pablo handed me my bag and I just stood there, awestruck by this example of generosity. I don't know how long I continued to stand there after his modest car drove away.

Living generously is one of the most important lessons we can demonstrate for the next generation. How generous are you? Are you willing to be more generous? Close your eyes for a moment and reflect on the ripple effect of uncomfortable generosity.

Not So Brilliant in the Basics

Just 7 years later? How could things change so drastically in just 7 years? I stared at the British sailor in disbelief. Did he really just say what I thought he said? Why was this a secret? Everyone should hear this. In one way or another, everyone has.

I was on a famous sailing ship in Portsmouth, England. Many of the D-Day invasion force launched from this port, just across the channel from Normandy. The dry docked ship I was touring gained its fame from another battle over a century before D-Day. Sailors on this famous old wooden ship were brilliant in the basics. But just seven years later, they were not. In 1805, the HMS Victory was part of the fleet that beat the Spanish and French in the Battle of Trafalgar, effectively demonstrating worldwide British Naval superiority.

The British sailor was a tour guide on the ship and told me that he rarely shares this story with Americans. He made me promise not to tell any other Americans. Okay, I made that up! The commander, Lord Horatio Nelson was fanatical about the basics. As a result, so was the crew. It took 10 or 15 men to fire each gun (at sea they call them guns, not cannons) and reload. And like clockwork every 60 to 90 *seconds*, each of the Victory's 104 guns would fire another shot. On the other hand, the French and Spanish at Trafalgar fired each of their guns every 6 to 10 *minutes*.

Nelson was killed on the deck by a sharpshooter during the battle and just seven years later the British and the Americans faced off in the War of 1812. But at that point, the numbers were completely flip-flopped. The Americans navy were firing each gun every 60 to 90 seconds, while the British fired every 6 to 10 minutes. In 1805, the British had become the world's dominant naval power. But, in my tour guide's words, the British Navy had become fat dumb and happy. They were once brilliant in the basics. Just seven years later they were not.

Brilliant in the basics – or not?

When hiring a new employee, you communicated expectations with brilliance, but perhaps that clarity of expectation has faded.

When you first were involved in running a meeting, coaching a sport, teaching a class, being a parent – you likely pursued brilliance in the basics…

When first dating your spouse, you were probably brilliant in the basics and then a few years went by...

Is it time to pick one area of your life and decide to once again become brilliant in the basics?

Maybe it's just in your morning routine, healthy eating habits, your approach to fitness. Perhaps it's one of these:

- the way you learn and study
- how you pay attention other people
- the passion in your communications
- the way you ask questions
- how you wait once you ask a question to engage others, to give them a chance to answer, to let them know that you want to hear their ideas

Become brilliant in the basics again.

There's a massive gap between being pretty good… and being brilliant in the basics. Where are you pretty good right now but it's time to become brilliant?

Great Communicator Secrets

Visiting a presidential library can be an incredibly exciting way to spend an afternoon, or even a few days – or it can be quite boring! That all depends on what you are looking for. Years ago, I read something from Ralph Waldo Emerson that has remained with me. Emerson wrote, "Every man I meet is my superior in some way, and in that I learn from him." If we visited any presidential library with this mindset, we just might be astounded by what we learn. Even just going through one ordinary day with this attitude has the potential to radically impact our lives. What have you learned from one of your family members recently? What about a stranger? I have given speeches and workshops in 49 of the 50 states (perhaps 50 by the time you read this) and on 3 continents. I often enter a leg of my travels with Emerson's words in my mind. I imagine that my Uber driver has a few great lessons to share, or that the person sitting next to me on the plane does. I had the chance to share the stage with Buffalo Bills quarterback and hall of famer, Jim Kelly. On my return flight from that keynote, my seatmate was a grandmother returning from a visit with her grandkids. I asked her what parenting lesson she wishes she had learned much earlier. "If you don't like the way your kids are turning out, take a good hard look in the mirror… and then make some changes!" She continued, "We have this tendency to want to blame their friends, their school, the media… Look in the mirror and make some changes!" If we ask and expect, how often will we find? Just a few days ago, I was facilitating a leadership retreat and asked a few of the organizers: "What was a profound lesson you learned about yourself recently?" The answers were amazing and incredibly insightful.

California's Simi Valley, just Northwest of Los Angeles, is home to the library for the 40th president of the United States.

The Great Communicator

Suppose you were pursuing the question along the lines of "How can I become a more engaging and memorable conversationalist?" Collecting one-liners, stories, and meaningful humorous stories might be a strategy to employ. Ronald Reagan was often referred to as *The Great Communicator*. Will we allow one of Reagan's habits to challenge our approach to communication? John F. Kennedy, Abe Lincoln, and Thomas Edison shared a version of this habit. In the Reagan Presidential Library, just north of Los Angeles, is an excellent example of his approach. Ronald Reagan had a large stack of three by five notecards with several one-liners and notes for stories on each card. He continuously added to the cards and would flip through them when preparing for a speech, interview, dinner, meeting, or press conference. Reagan was constantly collecting different ways to communicate. Thomas Edison did the same and would often review his note cards before or during interactions with important business contacts. Edison might leave the room, flip through cards in his coat pocket, and return with a great anecdote or joke to share. Have you ever interacted with someone who seems to be a brilliant conversationalist until you've heard their "spiel" a few times? What if that person followed this strategy?

An example of Reagan's method in action comes via a memorable leadership lesson that Colin Powell likes to share. Powell was in the Oval Office conversing with Reagan one on one. The president was seated in a chair by the fireplace while Powell explained the details of problem within his department. Powell stopped because, in his own words: "I realize he's paying no attention to me whatsoever. He's looking over my shoulder into the Rose Garden." Powell raised his voice to no avail. Powell spoke even louder, but the president continued looking out the window. Powell explained more details of his challenge until the president pointed out the window and said, "Colin! Colin! Look! Look! The squirrels just came and got the nuts I put in the Rose Garden!" With that, the meeting came to an end. A frustrated Colin Powell walked out of the Oval Office. Later that afternoon Powell realized what he described as the "brilliance of Ronald Reagan." In Powell's words: "Then it struck me, and it was something that I knew all along, but he crystallized it for me. Reagan was saying, 'Colin, I love you and I will sit here as long as you want me to, letting you tell me your problems. You let me know when I have a problem, and then I won't be looking at the squirrels in the Rose Garden.'" Powell considered Reagan an incredible leader, one who surrounded himself with talented leaders, empowered them to do their jobs, and then trusted them explicitly. In a conversation months later, when Reagan reminded him of some of the substance of the "squirrel" meeting, Powell realized Reagan had been listening intently after all. Perhaps the question Reagan pursued was along the lines of: "How can I communicate this lesson in a way that will truly stick?" or "What would be a fun way to help Colin see that he doesn't need my help with this?"

Enjoy a sampling of Reagan's one-liners, stories, and jokes:

- If we love our country, we should also love our countrymen.
- How can a president not be an actor?
- But there are advantages to being elected President. The day after I was elected, I had my high school grades classified Top Secret.
- I always wondered what the 10 Commandments would look like if Congress got their hands on them.
- People keep bringing up my age... *Thomas Jefferson said never judge a president by his age, only by his work...* Ever since he told me that, I've stopped worrying! Just to show you how youthful I am, I intend to campaign in all thirteen states.
- It has been said that politics is the second oldest profession. I have learned that it bears a striking resemblance to the first.
- As long as there are final exams, there will be prayer in school.

- [Inaugural Address, after quoting George Washington] For our friends in the press who place a high premium on accuracy, let me say I did not actually hear George Washington say that.
- Government's 1st duty is to protect the people, not run their lives.
- Freedom is never more than 1 generation away from extinction. We didn't pass it to our children in the bloodstream. It must be fought for, protected, and handed on for them to do the same.
- *Doveryai, no proveryai.* [Trust, but verify! – this comes from an ancient Russian proverb and Reagan loved to say it when talking about Russian relations, especially with Gorbachev.]
- There are no easy answers, but there are simple answers. We must have the courage to do what we know is morally right.
- Government is like a baby. An alimentary canal with a big appetite at one end and no sense of responsibility at the other.
- People who think a tax boost will cure inflation are the same ones who believe another drink will cure a hangover.
- Congress' biggest job: How to get money from the taxpayer without disturbing the voter.
- Three ways to get something done: Do it yourself; hire someone to do it; or forbid your kids to do it.
- Why can't life's problems hit us when we are 18 and know everything?
- We used to talk about our problems over cigarettes and coffee. Now cigarettes and coffee ARE our problems.
- If at first you don't succeed, do it the way she told you.
- Money may not buy friends, but it will help you to stay in contact with your children.
- The younger generation has no faults that being a parent and a taxpayer will not eliminate.
- There's little danger of our government being overthrown – there's too much of it.

- If you dread getting old because you won't be able to do the things you want to do, don't worry -- when you get older you won't want to do them.
- Government's view of the economy could be summed up in a few short phrases: If it moves, tax it. If it keeps moving, regulate it. And if it stops moving, subsidize it.
- If we ever forget that we are One Nation Under God, then we will be a nation gone under.
- There are no constraints on the human mind, no walls around the human spirit, no barriers to our progress except those we ourselves erect.
- Recession is when a neighbor loses his job. Depression is when you lose yours.
- The problem is not that people are taxed too little, the problem is that government spends too much.
- My fellow Americans, I am pleased to tell you I just signed legislation which outlaws Russia forever. The bombing begins in five minutes.
- Status quo, you know, is Latin for "the mess we're in".
- Some people wonder all their lives if they've made a difference. The Marines don't have that problem.
- [Notice the iterations: 5%!] No government ever voluntarily reduces itself in size. Government programs, once launched, never disappear. Actually, a government bureau is the nearest thing to eternal life we'll ever see on this earth!
- There is no such thing as a "temporary" government program.
- Governments tend not to solve problems, only to rearrange them.
- Government does not solve problems; it subsidizes them.
- The nine most terrifying words in the English language are: I'm from the government and I'm here to help.
- Welfare's purpose should be to eliminate the need for its own existence.
- We are a nation that has a government – not the other way around.

- Politics is not a bad profession. If you succeed there are many rewards, if you disgrace yourself you can always write a book.
- Concentrated power has always been the enemy of liberty.
- A people free to choose will always choose peace.
- Above all, we must realize that no arsenal, or no weapon in the arsenals of the world, is so formidable as the will and moral courage of free men and women. It is a weapon our adversaries in today's world do not have.
- Democracy is worth dying for, because it's the most deeply honorable form of government ever devised by man.
- People do not make wars; governments do.
- Protecting the rights of even the least individual among us is basically the only excuse the government has for even existing.
- Government always finds a need for whatever money it gets.
- How do you tell a communist? Well, it's someone who reads Marx and Lenin. And how do you tell an anti-Communist? It's someone who understands Marx and Lenin.
- If the Soviet Union let another political party come into existence, they would still be a one-party state, because everybody would join the other party.
- The Commissar visited a collective farm to see how the harvest was doing. When asked, a farmer said, "Oh comrade commissar! If we took all the potatoes, they would reach the foot of God."
The commissar replied, "Comrade farmer, this is the Soviet Union. There is no God"
The farmer replied, "That's okay. There are no potatoes."
- It's hard to get an automobile in the Soviet Union. They are owned mainly by elite bureaucrats. It takes an average of 10 years to get a car. 1 out of 7 families own automobiles. You have to go through a major process and put the money out in advance. After one man signed the paperwork for a car, the dealer said, "Okay in 10 years come get your car."
"Morning or afternoon?" said the man.

"Well, what difference does it make?" replied the dealer.

The man's reply: "The plumber is coming in the morning."

- Two men, an American and a Russian, were arguing. One said, "In my country I can go to the White House, walk to the president's office, pound on the desk, and say, 'Mr. President! I don't like how you're running things in this country!'"

  The Russian said, "I can do that too!"

  "Really?"

  "Yes! I can go to the Kremlin, walk into the general secretary's office and pound the desk and say, 'Mr. Secretary, I don't like how Reagan is running his country!'"

- Castro was making a speech to a large assembly. Someone out in the crowd said, "Peanuts! Popcorn! Crackerjack!" This happened about 4 times. Castro gets annoyed and says, "The next man who says that gets deported to Miami." The entire crowd stands up and yells, "POPCORN! PEANUTS! CRACKERJACK!"

- 3 men, a Frenchmen, a Brit and a Russian are at a museum looking at a portrait of Adam and Eve. The Brit says, "Adam and Eve are British. They wear fig leaves and blush so they must be modest." The Frenchman says, "No, they are French because they are naked and in love." The Russian said, "You're both wrong. They are obviously Russian. They are naked, have only an apple to eat and yet they are told they live in paradise."

- Mr. Gorbachev, tear down this wall!

Your Turn

Will you collect one-liners, quotes, and anecdotes? Will you add a new quote, question, or story each day or week? Will you test and tweak them in different situations and with different audiences? Will you tweak the beginning of your stories to capture attention? Five percent the length of your communications, the verbiage, the tone, the pauses, the emphasis, the humor. Notice from the long list above that Reagan iterated, created versions of similar statements.

I was once on the board of a non-profit with a great communicator. He was a master at buying attention. He would listen patiently as issues were discussed, but when he was ready to make a point or challenge the discussion, he typically leaned forward to get the group's attention. Then he would say something along the lines of, "We seem to be avoiding two crucial questions." Then he silently waited for someone to ask what the two questions were. Similar tactics helped him arouse curiosity over and over again so that he could share a perspective the group might be missing.

Will you become more creative in your communications?

Harvard of the Underclass: Saving Souls for Free

Would you eat dinner in a restaurant that considered itself the "Harvard of the Underclass"? Imagine this... you are seated in a San Francisco Bay restaurant along the Embarcadero with a great view of the Bay Bridge and have just decided on the meal you will order. *I ordered buttermilk chicken at the very enthusiastic recommendation of my waiter.* As you close the menu, the back cover catches your attention. It is the story of the restaurant, a story that captivates you. After the incredibly knowledgeable and polite waiter stops at your table, he asks if there will be anything else. Your facial expression catches his attention, so he waits for your question. You point to the back of the menu and ask if it is real.

He laughs and says, "Yes!"

You continue the question: "But not everyone who works here?"

"Everyone."

You are baffled. "No... really?"

"Yes, really."

"You, too?" You lean away from the table and shake your head in disbelief.

"Oh yes, me too. Definitely me."

You exchange smiles and he walks away to take care of your meal order. A fellow restaurant patron is perplexed and asks, "What was that all about?"

You point to the back of the menu and read a few highlights aloud. Every single one of the restaurant's staff is recovering from a life of crime and addiction: drugs, alcohol, gangs, prostitution, violence, theft, murder. A few moments after you read the words, you realize that you've temporarily forgotten to continue breathing.

181

> "Delancey Street is an incredible mix of hard practicality and idealism. It is the most successful program I've studied in the world."
>
> ~ Dr. Karl Menninger

This experience has been repeated thousands of times and is but a small example of the ripple effect started by a dream that Mimi Silbert was wise enough – or crazy enough – to pursue. About twenty minutes into my dining experience, Mimi, one of the most energetic people I have ever met, approached my table. She told me how happy she was to meet me and we hugged. Then she laughed and said something that shocked me. "How are all my nightmares treating you?" She wore an infectious smile and, as she said it, she spun around with her arms gesturing to all the restaurant staff. Then she apologized for messing up and promised to fix it. She continued, "That's what we do here. We mess up. But we fix it. We fix it. But then we mess up again. But that's okay, because we can fix it again. We get really good at fixing our mistakes."

I could only laugh because they hadn't messed anything up. I had called Delancey Street to try to arrange a tour just a few days earlier, but they were unable to accommodate my request. They did call me back several times and were about as polite in every interaction as I've ever experienced. Mimi smiled again and said, "Whenever you're ready for that tour, Vinnie will take you around. Then, if you have time, please come back so you and I can talk." Then she was gone. Did I hear Mimi correctly? Was I going to get to spend time with the incredibly creative woman who had started this whole operation?

Sometimes the answers are right in front of us. And they're not incredibly complicated. It's just that they are very hard to do. They require the payment of a deeply personal price. Mimi Silbert understood this... more than understood – lived – this. Margaret Meade said, "Never doubt that a small group of thoughtful, committed individuals can change the world. Indeed, it is the only thing that ever has." Mimi Silbert's life has been a picture of commitment, thoughtful creativity, and willingness to pay a deeply personal price that has changed the world for tens of thousands of people.

What does Mimi do?

What is this Delancey Street, this "Harvard of the Underclass," that proudly serves "the bottom 1%" of society?

The average resident is a third-generation gang member, has spent over a decade in prison and a dozen years addicted to drugs. Over 20,000 graduates demonstrate a track record unheard of in the rehabilitation field.

Mimi Silbert is the 95-pound dynamo behind Delancey Street's success and has been honored by organizations around the world. When she was honored as U.C. Berkeley Alumni of the Year, fellow recipients included many Nobel Prize winners, Gordon Moore (co-founder of Intel and author of Moore's law), Steve Wozniak (co-founder of Apple), Don Fisher (co-founder of the Gap clothing company), and Eric Schmidt (CEO of Alphabet, parent company of Google). If you ranked the UC Berkeley Alumni of the Year by net worth or annual income, Mimi might be at the bottom. But if you ranked by net impact, her position on that list would change dramatically. Dressed in formal attire, many of Delancey's residents accompanied her to the award dinner. After her brief speech, Silbert said "This beautiful thing [award] you've given me belongs to the residents of Delancey Street, and there is one person at each of your tables. [Until this moment, these diners identities were secret] Yes, they are former gang members, armed robbers, prostitutes, etc. These people have carried on intelligent conversations with you. Would our people please stand?" When the Delancey People stood, the rest of the diners not just applauded, but gave them a standing ovation. As Mimi describes it, "It's extraordinary how much people are moved by someone's ability to change, because if people with that level of anger and hatred can change, then the world can change."

"She's just amazing. She's the one that I can respect and call my mom."
~ A very common sentiment from many Residents

For Delancey Street's 30th anniversary, they decided to have a prom. Most of their tens of thousands of alumni have never finished high school and had never attended a prom. As the calls and letters went out to invite the alumni, they also found that most of the alumni weren't just regular citizens, they were also involved in significant community service, like church pancake breakfasts, helping at-risk youth, volunteering at soup kitchens, and much more. The habit of paying if forward stuck. How would you measure that ripple effect? It sounds like a miracle and I believe it is. Career criminals transforming into stand-out citizens.

I had the honor of spending several hours with Mimi. At one point, I asked, "Mimi, what happens with Delancey in 100 years, or 50 years... when there's no Mimi?"

She didn't seem worried about it at all. She explained that there are many, many people in each Delancey location that will keep it going. She laughed out loud when explaining that no one person would be crazy enough to get involved in all the things she does, but that would be okay. They wouldn't have to.

I told her how amazing it was to see all the little pieces that worked together to consistently perform miracles in the lives of people who were on society's rag pile. If you've ever read Og Mandino's wonderful stories about rag-pickers, you understand.

Mimi got quite serious for a moment and explained that she is not a planner, never has been. She let me know that she has always tried things. Most of the "things" didn't work out the way she thought they would, but she would keep trying and wasn't afraid to get rid of ideas that weren't working. That prom event... it was just an idea. Let's try it. So they did. Another infectious smile took over her face as she recounted something they had been trying for the last three years. She animatedly described some type of mini-tribal meeting experiment, waving her arms above her head before abruptly dropping them to her side with finality and modestly commenting, "We'll stop that experiment. It *really* didn't work." At the age of 75 and with the best re-hab program in the world, she was still trying things, still "messing up" and fixing it!

Mimi: "I don't know what else to call it but the Harvard of the underclass. This is a place where you come to live as a last chance when you're poor, you've been in prison, you've been using, everything – you've left school in the fifth grade. Many can't read or drive a car. It's a place where people come when nothing has gone right – often for several generations. Many have grandmothers who were in gangs."

Business meetings in the $20 million, 400,000 square foot complex in San Francisco Bay's Embarcadero may look rather ordinary, but at times Mimi will point out with her secretary did 12 years in prison for forgery and narcotics possession, or that the head of the moving company spent almost 2 decades in San Quentin State Prison!

How? Mimi's Journey

Tough Love. Each one teach one. You are needed. Act as if. You are responsible.

Let's make the program free. Not just free to participate, but free room and board, as well. Let's do all this with no staff and no government funding. No therapists. No professional staff. No donations, no grants, no guards—just a remarkable influence strategy that has profoundly changed the lives of tens of thousands of people over almost fifty years. Recidivism – relapse – rates for U.S. programs outside Delancey: 77% fall off the wagon. Inside

Delancey, over 90% never go back to drugs or crime. Instead, they earn degrees, become professionals, and change their lives. Forever.

> **"If our residents don't become talented very quickly, then we don't eat.... If we do well, we all eat steak. If not, we all eat rice and beans."** *Mimi Silbert*

Mimi says, "We started out with the idea that we would not be funded ... we wanted to teach our residents to earn money so that everything the organization achieved, the residents would know it was they who achieved it." Since day one, Mimi has lived among the residents, eaten meals with them, worked side by side with them. She takes no salary.

If you're anything like me, you have to be wondering several things. Is this real? Does it actually work? It must fall apart on a regular basis. If it actually works, what are their secrets. Well, it is real, it does work, not without hiccups, and they have many secrets to share with the world. Mimi has been relentlessly pursuing the question: "How do we build a place that actually works and is self-funded?" Throughout the journey, she has been willing to experiment, to try things, to fail, to humbly ask what lessons each experiment or failure carries, to believe in people even though they don't always appreciate it or reciprocate that hope.

How is this possible? Mimi Silbert was a therapist early in her career. One day, she walked out of a counseling session and the patient said, "Thank you for helping me." Mimi's first thought was, "Wow! Mimi, you're a good girl! You're doing good things!" And then it hit her like a ton of bricks. Everyone needs that feeling. Every person on the planet needs to feel like they are serving, like they are adding value to another person, like they are needed. She realized that maybe the best way for her to help other people would be to help them help other people. That was part of the seed that became Delancey Street.

It started very small, in a San Francisco apartment in the early 1970's, but the pursuit of different questions and willingness to learn from many mistakes led to something incredible. Silbert's typical "new hires" have had four felony convictions. They've been homeless for years, and most are lifetime drug addicts. Within hours of joining Delancey, they are working in one of Delancey's many businesses, which include a restaurant, moving company (just imagine having all your belongings packed up by ex-felons who know the grounds of San Quentin... By the way, the San Francisco branch of the moving company is the largest independent moving firm in Northern California), automotive repair, Christmas tree lots, wood furniture making, limo service (with clients including Gap, William Sonoma, and Pottery Barn), digital printing, and ironworks. Currently, Delancey Street operates in five locations with over twenty businesses and generates over $20 Million in annual revenue.

> **"If somebody gave you 35 prisoners, and they moved into your house, you'd say, 'You'll all have to help out because I'm certainly not doing your laundry. Who wants to be head of laundry?' You wouldn't sit there yourself trying to run them all." Mimi Silbert**

Their first business enterprise came about accidentally. A young resident wanted to go back to finish high school and they looked for a private school that would take a barter. In exchange, one school said you have to paint the school and build a small playground set for the younger children. No one at Delancey knew how to paint so they read a few books about painting. They disassembled and reassembled the playground set six times! At first, the children came off the slide and launched into the air because something was attached incorrectly. Disassemble. Rebuild!

As this "extended family" at Delancey grew, they moved out of the small apartment into an abandoned 40 room mansion in San

Francisco's Pacific Heights. They bought the building for just $50,000, but it needed a lot of work, so they applied the lessons learned from painting the school and building the children's playground towards renovating the entire building. When completed, it was one of the nicest buildings in the neighborhood, but their neighbors were not thrilled to have 100 violent felons moving next door. To make sure that crime went down instead of up, Delancey Street residents became the crime patrol for the neighborhood. They also visited every single neighbor, volunteered their services, and told them that they wanted an opportunity to prove that they would be the best neighbors.

> **"When you don't take any government money, you can do what you believe in deep in your belly." Mimi Silbert**

But could they succeed? Aren't habitual behaviors tough to change? Delancey Street has learned that they need to focus on just two behaviors, not dozens, to open the floodgates for substantial and lasting change. Silbert explains that, "The hardest thing we do here is try to get rid of the code of the street. It says: 'Care only about yourself, and don't rat on anyone.' If you reverse those two behaviors, you can change everything else." To reverse these ingrained habits, Delancey requires 1) each person to take responsibility for someone else's success and 2) that everyone confront everyone else about every single violation. It sounds simple, but residents include Crips, Bloods, neo-Nazis, white supremacists, prostitutes, Mexican Mafia members, and lifetime drug addicts. And they're all bunking together! As you might imagine, tensions can run high.

> **"I thought everyone had former pimps and prostitutes picking them up at school." David Silbert (Mimi's son)**

The Journey of a New Resident

Applicants must submit a written request for acceptance into Delancey Street, go through an interview panel with current residents, and promise to stay in the program at least two years completely drug and alcohol free and nonviolent. Whenever someone new arrives, two Delancey residents interview the person. The new applicant tells their story and in Mimi's words, "we interrupt. We try to get you to stop blaming everyone. If you are hung up on your mother, we say, 'If your mother controls your life and you want your life to be different, why don't you send your mother here and will work with her because obviously you have nothing to do with your own life.' We try to get the person to admit that *they* did not make me pull the trigger, *they* did not make me rip the purse from the old lady. Yes, I did it."

The new resident is assigned a dorm room and a dorm head. Someone who's been there for a month or so who will explain all the rules (they joke about having 999 rules!): get up in the morning, make your bed, do your dorm duties, take a shower. New residents *immediately* begin working a full 8 to 5 day with school work afterwards.

> **"New residents long for prison, where virtually nothing is expected of them." Mimi Silbert**

Each new resident is also assigned to a Minyan, named after the Jewish prayer quorum. The roughly ten members of each Minyan can be extremely diverse, including skinheads, gang members, and prostitutes of every race, creed, and nationality.

The 10 are told, "one little tiny piece of you wants to change or you wouldn't have come here, so it's up to the 10 of you to help each other turn that little thing of hope into a real hope."

Anytime one of them in the group of 10 does anything wrong, all 10 will be called together and asked why it was done and why no one reported it. The only form of punishment is washing dishes.

Within the first week, each resident is placed in charge of someone else. From that time forward, they're not asked how they are doing. Instead, they are asked how their crew is doing. While the regular work days 8 to 5, Mimi likes to say they live life with the tape recorder. Every half hour or so they'll press the pause button to give feedback, encouragement, or learning. During a morning pause, a resident might conduct a seminar with a single vocabulary word or a concept. The lesson could be a quote from Emerson that they all discuss. Everybody checks everybody else all day with the vocabulary word or quote. At noon that talk about current events or review books. They may press pause to practice setting a table, choosing work outfits, or tying a tie. Every day, residents dress for and attend dinner where they all sit and chat. Most residents have never sat down at a family table for dinner. Twice a week they get together in groups to release stuffed emotions and they try to laugh at themselves constantly.

> **"We teach people who are used to being self-centered and full of hate to become full of love and to take care of each other. We give no therapy because the only therapy that works is to forget about yourself for a while and worry about somebody else." Mimi Silbert**

A Few Life Guidelines:

A few of Delancey Street's mantras would transform any organization – if that organization would truly live them. These core behaviors correlate with reversing the street code *"Care only about yourself, and don't rat on anyone."* As mentioned earlier, violators are subject to extra work, such as washing dishes.

• Each one teach one.

• Care for each other – be both a giver and a receiver.

• Take responsibility for your actions; recognize that everything you do impacts others. Own up to your mistakes and simply fix them.

• Act "as if" you can become a decent, talented person of integrity (with the expectation that in doing so, you will eventually become one).

Lessons in the Small Things

Mimi says, "New people are comfortable in the world of drugs, hate, failure, and they bring that with them even though they know it's self-destructive. You'll have a new person say, I got the crappy broom, that's why I did a bad job. 'But c'mon,' I'll say to the person, 'You've been doing this your whole life. You've got to learn to work with what you've got, to work with one another.' They've lived a life of looking for other people to blame."

Act As If

My tour guide repeated the phrase over and over. It was part of his vernacular. "I as if'd it." "I remember my first time waiting tables and dealing with restaurant customers – I just as if'd it!" When I asked what this expression meant, he leaned forward, with a look of excitement to be able to teach me something. He had already taught this to dozens and dozens of his peers at Delancey. He explained that we all "as if" things. When we're little, we might not really know how to hit a baseball, so we act as if we do. We stand like our father, our big sister, or a professional baseball player, and we hold the bat as if we did know how to hit. We put on our uniforms as if we were serious ball-players. He said that when he was getting involved in drugs, he didn't really know how to be in that environment, so he "as if'd" it He didn't know how to be homeless, so he "as if'd" it. He said "now – here – we as if good things instead of bad things. We "as if" we have a great attitude. We 'as if' we like interacting with the restaurant customers. We "as if" we are professional. We "as if" good stuff until it becomes real." He explained that it's like layers. You act as if on the outside long enough until that 'as if' sinks into who you really are.

Residents are continuously taught, "Act as if... Act as if you really care. You might not feel it, but act as if you care about helping another person. The first step for a newcomer is to get out of yourself, to stop thinking about yourself and worry about another."

Newcomers want to leave, but even though they're not really feeling it, they encourage other newcomers not to leave because they're taught by fellow residents to talk that way. But all of a sudden one day they feel, "No, no, don't give up. If you give up, we all give up." And suddenly they feel it.

What if you and I did this a bit more often? "As if" you're an incredible husband or wife. "As if" you want to have a great relationship with *that* person. "As if" your standards were higher. "As if" you were a successful entrepreneur. "As if" you had courage. "As if" you cared more than is safe. "As if" you were more creative. "As if" it is your time to lead.

Each One Teach One

Each one teach can be applied to most valuable life lessons. Those who can read at the 8th grade level teach others who are at the 6th grade level, who teach others at the 4th or 5th grade level. Someone who is learning that it's better not to lie, even about little things would then teach this lesson forward to someone who might not yet have learned it. The residents joke about the 999 basic rules because they say that it starts with everything, even down to the details of how to make your bed, fold your clothes, and set and clear the table for meals. Most of the residents need to learn just about everything related to living a normal life.

Mimi says, "...we rely on the people who have the problems to become their own solution. We do that by something we call, 'Each one teach one, and each one help one.' Our average resident is now a third-generation gang member. They've gone in and out of prison, basically, their whole lives. They even have grandmothers in gangs. Society is always worried about what we can do for them to get them to stand up, to be stronger and healthier, but at Delancey Street we need them. When you have no staff and you have no funding, you need the people in your extended family. We've run it like an extended family, you need them to rise up to be the best of themselves and give to each other."

> "No one should be in the position of only receiving, because it would make you powerless, useless, and give you a victim's view of life... Every resident is both a teacher and a learner, a giver and a receiver. And it's really in the giving and in the teaching that most people change." Mimi Silbert

You Are Needed

Mimi: "The word [rehabilitation] is funny to me because most were never '*habilitated*' to begin with. They come here, and for some weird reason, we love them and we believe in them and they run the place."

Each resident must also develop three marketable skills, one in each of these categories: physical (hands on), retail (customer interaction), and computer (often finance). These roles are learned within the dozens of businesses operated under the Delancey umbrella.

Abe Irizarry *"graduated"* from every California prison, was once a member of the Mexican Mafia, and vividly recalls part of his own personal transition: "I kept saying I'd leave, but after a while, it struck a chord in me. I wanted to be somebody." Today,

Abe serves as Vice President of the Delancey Street Foundation and supervises intake interviews of new residents.

Even visitors are given a tour by residents. Mimi described one of the tour guides who used to be an active skinhead: "His entire body is covered with tattoos of swastikas and other symbols of hate and violence. My goal isn't to shock tourists but to help them understand why crimes of hatred and vengeance take place."

The Delancey Street population have spent most of their lives as takers. The game changes as they learn to become givers, learn how to serve before they think they deserve. Mimi believes that imprisoning criminals "at someone else's expense, providing all their food and lodging and letting them sit there with no responsibility, is absurd. If you care about people, you hold them accountable." I asked Mimi, what's the biggest change in your approach over the decades of doing this incredible work? "Today, I love them more than ever. And I'm tougher on them." Mimi's bold love pumps through the veins of Delancey Street and brings the words of Saint Augustine of Hippo to life: "The greatest kindness one can render to any man is leading him to truth."

Annual Christmas Party

At 4'11", Mimi Silbert dresses as Santa for the family Christmas party with about 500 family members at the San Francisco location. She knows the back story on every single resident as well as their shoe size! Why? Each new Delancey resident gets a Christmas present that includes the most professional clothing most have ever owned. It's often their first experience of a family Holiday, and some shy away. But Mimi requires that they try on their new outfits and model them for everyone to see.

Individual personalities are kept in mind when assembling wardrobes. Flashier ties with swirling colors will go to those willing to wear them, but not to those who would want to show off in them.

Outfits are selected just on the edge of someone's attitude – to push them to be a bit bolder, or to teach them a bit more humility.

"Mimi teaches the principles of Christmas – that it's about giving," said former resident Mike DeLane, now a San Francisco fire captain. "She's like the mother nobody around here ever had." Another resident said that it isn't about the stuff in the box. "It's about being in that room on Christmas, to finally actually feel loved by people who are going to go through the hard time with you and truly love you no matter what." The way Mimi sees it, everyone at Delancey is an immigrant to mainstream society, just like her parents who fled Eastern Europe to escape the Nazis during World War II. They settled on Delancey Street in New York, pooled their money and eventually built a better life. Along the way, Mimi learned the value of sharing resources with her extended family.

> **"No matter who we used to be, it doesn't matter. She sees us for who we are now." My Delancey Street barista**

Resident Robert McCormick experienced his first Christmas at Delancey in 2008. "It's an amazing feeling. I finally felt what it must be like to have a family." Going from rags to Brooks Bros. was such an uplifting experience for 34-year-old Sean Cronk that he couldn't contain his tears remembering it. "All of a sudden people perceived me differently." Once, while at a hospital, the staff mistook him for a doctor. Sean said this moment of respect left a lasting mark on his soul.

A few Graduate Success Stories

"I had no morals, no values, no trust, no education, only took care of myself and didn't do that very well. I'm responsible now. I have goals. I want to help people. I'm going to become a nurse.... I learned how to be honest and dependable.... Thing I love about Delancey is helping the new people that come off the street. They were just like me. I get to watch them grow, watch them become responsible." Rena Williams (resident working at the restaurant)

Kim Barish learned design in Delancey's Christmas decorating department. She became a production designer at Foote, Cone & Belding.

Mike Delane had hit bottom as a crack addict. He became a captain in the San Francisco fire department; he also works to help kids stay off drugs.

Shirley LaMarr was involved with drugs and prostitution for 20 years, and had been in and out of jail. She went on to run social service programs including one in a prison.

Robert Rocha had committed 24 robberies and landed in San Quentin prison by the time he was 18 years old. After Delancey, he became a district sales manager for Pepsi, a husband and a father.

Bill Toliver went to school to study mortuary science while at Delancey. He became a medical examiner for the city of San Francisco.

Jimmy Tyrell had hit bottom with heroin. He got his general contractor's license while building Delancey's facility on the Embarcadero. He went on to run his own contracting business.

Billy Maher went through college and law school while at Delancey Street and as a graduate was elected President of the San Francisco Unified School District Board. His son Sean went on to study at Oxford University.

Pete Hopkins owns a trucking business and volunteers at Delancey Street's charter high school for at-risk students.

Jesse Senore came all the way from Maine to attend a Delancey reunion, has been running a successful business for over 20 years, and is putting his five daughters through college.

Charlie Haden is a world-renowned jazz bass player who is still playing around the world and has performed with Ringo Starr.

Mary Carouba is an investigative social worker in the Human Services Department in Sonoma County and does comedy routines in clubs and cruise ships around the world and has written a wonderful book, ***Women at Ground Zero: Stories of Courage and Compassion*** about the women impacted during the 9/11 attacks.

A committed lunatic!

There's not a single person in Mimi Silbert's life who didn't tell her that she was crazy to start such an organization. But, in her own words, "You need a strong, visionary, committed lunatic to dedicate a life to initiate something. To continue, Delancey Street must be bigger than I am…. We've done things we didn't know we could do because we didn't know we couldn't do them." As a child, Mimi scored in the 6th percentile in a mathematics aptitude test, meaning 94% of American children her age scored with a higher aptitude for mathematics than Mimi. Perhaps this was her greatest asset. As Mimi says, she didn't know what might not be possible!

I've now visited Delancey Street several times. During my daughters' first experience eating there, our waiter told us that he met his daughter when she turned 18 and visited him in prison. They now have a great relationship. My barista at the coffee shop on the other end of the complex saw me holding a book and said, "I love reading! What are you reading?" We chatted about books for a few minutes and I later wondered if she always loved books or if she was in the middle of an "as if" I love reading journey. Mimi once told me that the restaurant serves several functions, but she especially wants 1) to show the world who "we" can be and 2) help us see who the world can be.

Thank you, Mimi, and thank you to the wonderful thousands of Delancey Street graduates who are changing things!

Will you commit to something you don't know you can't do? What will it be? When will you start? What are you waiting for?

Where do YOU go from Here?

Where do you go from here? If you and I meet a few months from now, which of these 5 pillars will you have intentionally strengthened in your life?

A nurse took a few days off to recharge. She needed it and when she returned to the hospital, she was full of life. There was a new enthusiasm and energy coursing through her being. She practically danced through the halls and her words were like a song. She stopped in to see an elderly patient who hadn't been very active and rarely had a visitor. She ducked her head in and with a contagious smile said, "You have the best view – especially this time of day!" The man barely made eye contact but she walked into the room and made a bee-line straight for the curtains. As she pulled them wide open, she exclaimed, "Look at that! The way the sun reflects off the trees. All those colors. People drive for hours to see those colors and you've got them right here. How'd you get this room? You must have some good connections, eh?"

The man looked through the open curtains, smiled a faint smiled a faint smile and his eyes opened a bit wider.

The nurse thought to herself: *it's working!* Then she noticed an apple sitting on the table next to the man's hospital bed. "You know what they say… an apple a day…"

The man didn't finish the phrase, but you know it, don't you? The nurse was persistent and practically sang the words, "An aaaaaaaapple a daaaaaaaaaaay…." Now the man smiled a broad smile. He even laughed. The nurse was thrilled and gestured with her hands for him to finish the line. He chuckled and they sang it together, in not quite perfect harmony: "Keeeeeeeps the doctor awaaaayyy!" Then man laughed again and said, "You know, I think it's true. I haven't seen a doctor in here for maybe three, four days!"

It is true. Maybe not the story, but the apple affecting your health. That's true. We've all heard the expression, but it seems some of us change it up a little bit. A donut a day... A jug o' coffee a day... A bagel with cream cheese a day... A candy bar a day... The expression is so simple. And it has a positive impact. More than a positive impact, it creates a ripple effect that would be hard to measure. One slight change in a daily diet affects energy levels, focus, emotional control, patience, not to mention long-term health. We've all heard the expression but how many people do you know who eat an apple every day? Not so many.

So often, that's exactly how game-changers work. They're rarely big complicated ideas or strategies. Most game-changers are simple ideas that we actually act on. We build them into our lives. We let them affect us. I've spent much of my career in pursuit of game-changers. Looking for them, teaching them, helping organizations implement them, trying to apply them in my own life. And most of these game-changers are incredibly simple.

I ask again: Where do you go from here?

Do you ask a question a day? Do you collect or iterate an option a day? Try something where you might end up face first in the snow? Game-changers. Incredibly simple. Incredible impact.

These 5 pillars are game-changers. Practice any one of the five and it could be the start of a profound ripple effect in your world.

If you had to score yourself on each of the 5 (0 to 10 with 10 being consistently world-class), where do you score?

Ask.
Expect.
Collect.
Iterate.
F4(OB).

Again, which one will you intentionally practice over the next few days, weeks, months?

Leonardo da Vinci said, "Art is never finished, only abandoned." What does that mean for you and me? Get started. For an author, it means get it out there. Abandon something you've written to the readers. In some area of your life, add more creativity. Version one is better than version none! Walt Disney coined a phrase, "Plus it!" How can we plus it? Add to it, make it a little better, a little more magical? After Disneyland opened, Walt encouraged his staff to visit the park regularly, perhaps eating lunch there weekly. He wanted them to talk to guests and come back with ideas to plus the experience. Walt was there all the time. He would ask visitors what they loved and what they didn't. He carried a roll of cash, handing a $5 tip (~$55 today) to cast members who did something to plus the guest experience. He encouraged cast members to take 5 minutes every day to create a magical memory for a guest that might last a lifetime. Plus it! How can you plus your morning routine? Your Saturday morning breakfast? Your weekend with friends? Your Tuesday meeting? Your routine drives with the kids? The interview or new hire experience?

So many or our clients have created incredibly meaningful and memorable – yet often very simple – strategies to plus it for their customers and culture. One recent client asked, "How can we plus the work experience for our remote and part-time staff?" and created over 200 ideas on ways to plus the employee experience. They also iterated the question many times, including: "What are some simple but powerful ways to let our people know how much we value them?" and "Which can we do this afternoon?"

For many years now, my wife and I have been pursuing the question, "How can we spend a month each year in Europe?" Asking a good question is very different from pursuing that question. We all ask good questions now and then. We even ask great questions at times. But pursuing them… that's entirely different. We've spent a month in Poland, a month in Germany, a month in the UK, a month in Italy three times… As a Dad, I love to ask, "What are some simple experiences that could change the way my kids see the world and their role in it?" Pursue that question for a few days! During our most recent trip to Italy, we took the kids to the Da Vinci museum in Florence. It's an incredibly interactive museum where you can play with many of Da Vinci's inventions. That and some gelato plussed the visit to Florence! Walt Disney just might have handed us $5 for creating a meaningful memory that day.

Get started. You know that Maya Angelou was right: "You can't use up creativity. The more you use, the more you have."

You have an incredible innate potential for creativity. You also have an incredible ability to help unleash creativity in people around you. Recall George Land's study. At the age of 5, you were a creative genius. Over the next few years, you learned non-creative behavior. Can you re-learn that creative behavior? Absolutely. One of the biggest keys to behavior change is acting differently than you feel. Our habitual feelings around creativity are well-trained. We feel like being creative in pockets and moments. As you've been reading this book, I imagine that you've challenged that. You've expanded your mind. You've explored different questions.

My hope is that you've seen and experienced several things: 1) these ideas are not complicated – you can apply them in many ways, 2) world-class innovators simply apply them more often, more consistently, and maybe a bit better than most of us, and 3) it's worth intentionally unleashing more creativity in your world.

Leonardo da Vinci tells me that it's time to let it go. Release it. Abandon it to the world. I read Leonardo's words on one of those trips to Florence. I mentioned it earlier, but it's worth repeating:

"L'arte non è mai finita, solo abbandonata."
Art is never finished, only abandoned.

And so I abandon this book to you. Of course, I could change some things, but now it's your turn. Here's to the crazy ones... Here's to you. Change some things!

About the Author

Jonathan Fanning is the author of several books, including ***Who are you BECOMING?*** and ***I Once Was Lost***. He has inspired and challenged audiences with his message in 49 states and on 3 continents. Jonathan was voted the best speaker at a TEDx conference. He speaks for companies, non-profits, schools, parenting groups, and churches. A traumatic car accident and several other "Frying Pan" moments in the middle of Fanning's career as a management consultant launched a quest for a deeper sense of purpose, meaning, and significance. *"Who are you BECOMING?"* and *"Who are you helping the people around you to BECOME?"* became central to Jonathan's life, business, and speaking. He has built and operated several successful businesses, including a national children's fitness franchise and Entrepreneur Adventure, designed to help young people experience business start-up and ownership. Jonathan lives in NY with his amazing wife and two daughters.

Keynotes, workshops and coaching programs include:
- *Who are you BECOMING?*
- *Creativity Unleashed: 5 Habits of World-Class Innovators*
- *The Servant Leader Paradox: Leaders we Choose to Follow*
- *Developing Emotional Intelligence*

For more information, engaging videos, and thought-provoking content that compliments this book, visit us online:

www.JonathanFanning.com

Made in the USA
Middletown, DE
26 September 2023